# DISCOVER NIGERIA

Paula B Sofowora

amlap publishing

*This book is dedicated to Mum and Dad*

First published in 2008 by
Amlap Publishing
PO Box 6144
Basildon
Essex SS14 0WX

Printed in Belgium by Proost

Edited by Ruth Nason
Designed by Mark Graves at 432 Limited



ISBN 978-0-9546116-2-0

**Acknowledgements**

For their encouragement and support of her project to create this book, the author gives special thanks to her family: Femi, Remi and Seun Sofowora, John Onigbinde, Yemisi Onigbinde and Rebecca Ayanfalu. She is also very grateful to Funke Salako, Boma Ozobia, Dapo Segun, George Ajanlekoko, Pius Ekpei, Roger Wickham at Amherst Publishing, Segun Olayungbo, Simi Belo, Sunday Adogeri, Tunji Alawode, Tunde Busari, Yinka Essien, Jim Bax, Bridget Shine at IPG, Professor and Mrs Odeyemi, Patti Boulaye, Joanne Alexander, Sola Oyebade, Remi Odejinmi, Sade Olajubu, Toyin Salami, Sandra Teichman, Patricia Ogunfeibo, Dekanla Jackson, Sue Hanks, Felicia Laing, Akin Salami, Ropo Ewenla, Robin Blake at the Essex Enterprise Centre, Wale Onalapo, Bradley Snelling, Tony Tufnell, Tunde Ogunseitan, Verna Wilkins, Gloria Igbaji, Oby Osuchukwu, Thomas Ngoma and Seye Aina.

Thanks go to the following for their particular help with the content of the book: Anthony Adeloye at the Nigerian High Commission Library for help with general research; Dr Akin Oyetade, Godson Echebima and Dr Abba I. Tijani, Language Centre, School of Oriental and African Studies, University of London, for translations for the alphabet pages; Godson Echebima and Nkiru Aderanti for information on the Igbo; Dr Abba I. Tijani and Suleiman Mustafa for information on the Hausa; Dr Akin Oyetade, Buki Ogunyemi, Mrs Funke Sofowora and Mrs Onibokun for information on the Yoruba; Agnes Shodimu, Gbemi Olowolafe, Jayne Dear at Woodlands School, Jonathan Brough at City of London School for Girls, Jonathan Wickes at Chelmsford Library Headquarters, Toyin Oriade and Sharon Griffith for advice on the curriculum; Sue Hammond at Billericay School, Sue Pipe and Jenny Sampson at Great Berry School and Ade Omolaja for feedback on the book; Alan Minnis for his invaluable assistance on the maps; Anna and Sonya Minnis, Janet Sherlock, and Patricia Ford for help with checking proofs.

*Illustration and photograph acknowledgements are on page 62.*

# Contents

# A letter from the author

Dear Reader,

I am delighted that you have chosen to look at this book about Nigeria.

Perhaps you have met someone from Nigeria and you are interested to know some more about their country. Perhaps you are Nigerian yourself, or belong to a Nigerian family that moved to live in another country before you were born.

Like many other Nigerians, my parents moved to the UK in the 1960s. I was born in England, in 1964. When I was 10, my brother and I went to live in Nigeria. I then returned to the UK in 1985, after studying English and Literature at university. I am married and have two sons.

Several years ago. I looked for a book that would show my sons about Nigeria and their cultural heritage, something that they could share with their friends at school. I could not find what I wanted, and so I decided to research and write a book myself. I hope it will show you Nigeria in the 21st century, from a British Nigerian's perspective.

I think it is important for people to know more about Nigeria, not just because cultural heritage is something to be proud of and fully embraced, but also because Nigeria is the most populated country in Africa, potentially one of the wealthiest, and Nigerians are all over the place!

I believe it is really valuable to learn about each other's countries. In this book, you will find that learning about Nigeria also helps you to learn about the country where you live now. See what differences and similarities you can spot between Nigeria and your country, and try to answer some of the questions.

Happy reading!

Best wishes,

Paula B Sofowora

My mum, dad, brother and me, in the 1960s.

Me with my two sons, my husband and my mother-in-law, in about 1997. We are all dressed in traditional Nigerian outfits.

With my brother and sisters in 2006.

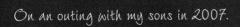

On an outing with my sons in 2007.

# The continent of Africa

Did you know that Africa covers more than one-fifth of the Earth's land surface? It is the second-largest of the Earth's seven continents and contains 53 countries. African people belong to a variety of fascinating cultures, and they speak more than 1,000 languages – a greater number than in any other continent.

## DO YOU KNOW?

Which continent do you live in: Africa, Europe, Asia, North America, South America, Australasia or Antarctica?

Is Europe bigger or smaller than Africa?

How many countries are there in Europe?

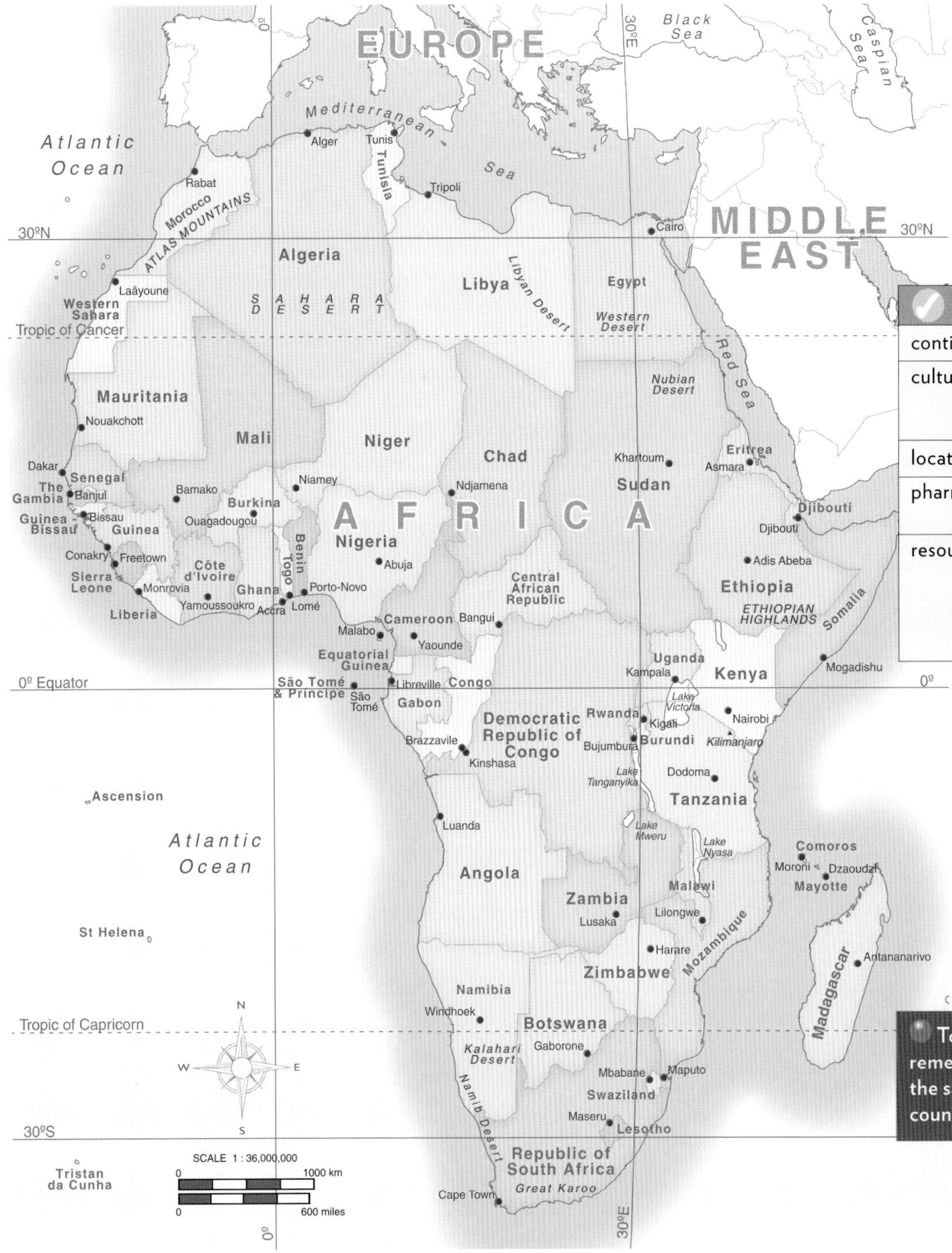

| ✔ WORD CHECK | |
|---|---|
| continent | a large landmass. |
| culture | a group in society with its own beliefs, values and traditions. |
| location | where something is. |
| pharmacist | an expert in providing drugs and medicine. |
| resource | something that is or can be useful or valuable; for example, good farming land, and materials that can be mined. |

To understand how big Africa is, remember that the UK is only about the same size as the West African country of Ghana.

SCALE 1 : 36,000,000

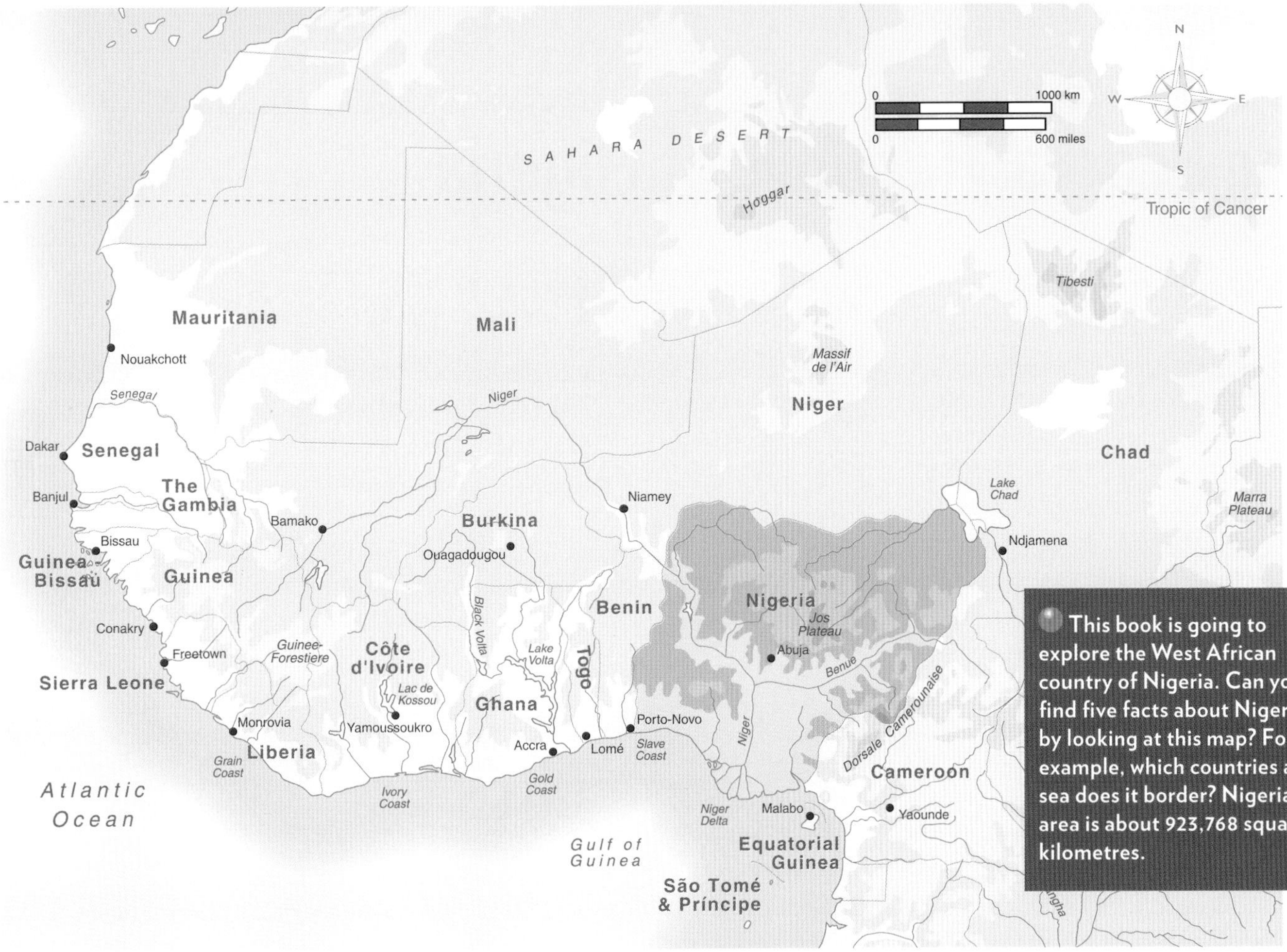


This book is going to explore the West African country of Nigeria. Can you find five facts about Nigeria, by looking at this map? For example, which countries and sea does it border? Nigeria's area is about 923,768 square kilometres.

# The heart of Africa

The Nile, the Congo and the Niger are the three longest rivers in Africa. You can see from the map above that the Niger runs through several countries in West Africa, including Nigeria. Nigeria is sometimes called the 'heart' of Africa, because of its location and its importance in terms of its people, its resources and its peace-keeping role in the continent.

What knowledge and ideas about Nigeria do you have, as you begin to read this book? What would you like to find out about Nigeria?

**EXPLORERS FROM EUROPE**

The first Europeans to visit Africa were Portuguese explorers in the 15th century. Some explorers tried to find the source of the River Nile and the River Niger. See if you can find out which British explorer made journeys along the River Niger in 1795-96 and 1805. Did he find its source?

Footballer Jay Jay Okocha and pharmacist Professor Dora Akunyilli are two Nigerians whose skills have made them known around the world. Which other famous Nigerian people can you think of? You will learn about many more from the quizzes at the end of this book.

# The Federal Republic of Nigeria

Nigeria's official name, the Federal Republic of Nigeria, tells you about its system of government. 'Federal' means made up of several states. Nigeria has 36 states, each with its own government to look after local affairs. There is also a main 'federal' government for the whole country. Each state receives a budget from the federal government, but some states are richer than others.

A republic is a country that does not have a king or queen or royal family. Instead, a republic has a leader, called the president, who is elected by the people. The President of Nigeria is Chief of State and Head of the Government.

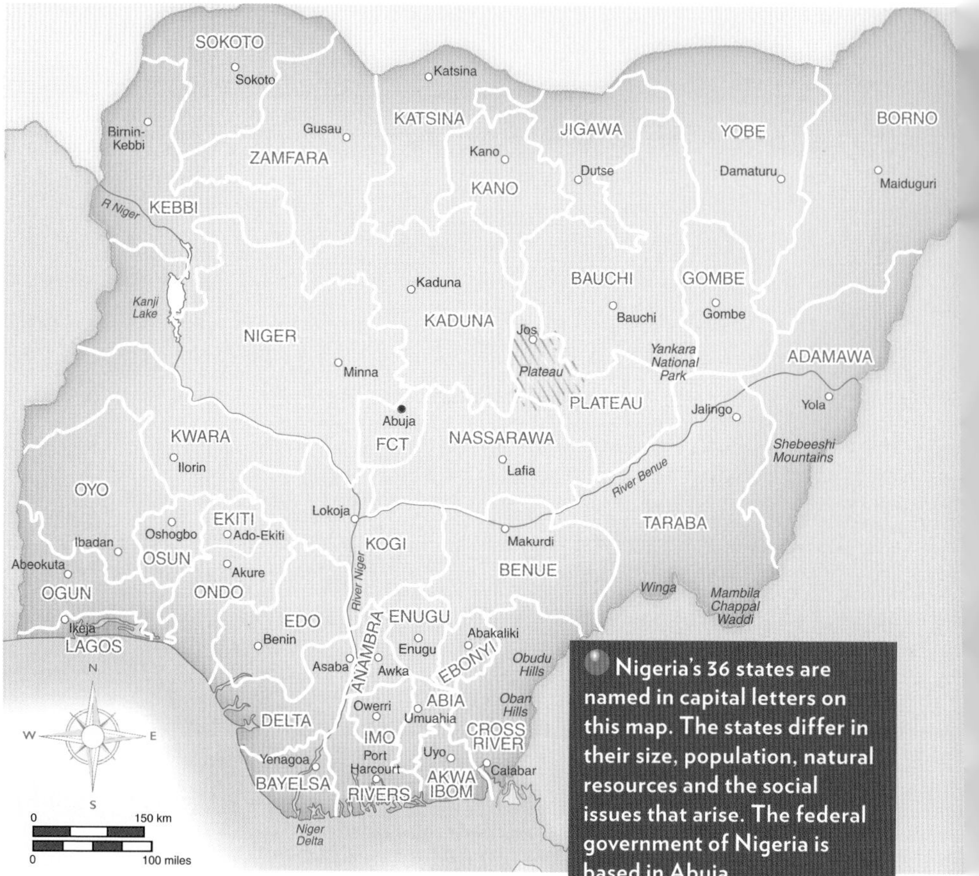


Nigeria's 36 states are named in capital letters on this map. The states differ in their size, population, natural resources and the social issues that arise. The federal government of Nigeria is based in Abuja.

Umaru Yar'Adua (below left) became President of Nigeria on 29 May 2007. Before that, he was governor of Katsina State.

## DO YOU KNOW?

Which other countries are federal republics?

What is the system of government in your country?

What other systems of government do you know?

| WORD CHECK | |
|---|---|
| budget | a sum of money that may be used for a particular purpose. |
| elect | to choose by voting. |
| estimate | to work out a possible figure, based on the facts available. |
| population | all the people living in a place. |
| social issues | problems affecting the people living in a place. |
| territory | an area of land. |
| urban | in or belonging to towns and cities. |

# Nigeria's capital

Until 1991, the capital of Nigeria was Lagos, on the coast of Lagos State. Then Abuja became the 'Federal Capital Territory', where the Nigerian government has its headquarters. Lagos is still the main port and centre of industry and trade.

The Three Arm Zone in Aso Rock, Abuja, is home to the National Assembly (right), the Supreme Court and the Presidential buildings.

## NIGERIAN CITIES

The majority of people in Nigeria live in large cities such as Lagos, Ibadan, Port Harcourt, Benin and Kaduna. In 2000 it was estimated that over 43.5% of Nigeria's population lived in urban centres, but that this would increase to more than 50% by 2010, as more and more people move to the cities to find employment or a better standard of living.

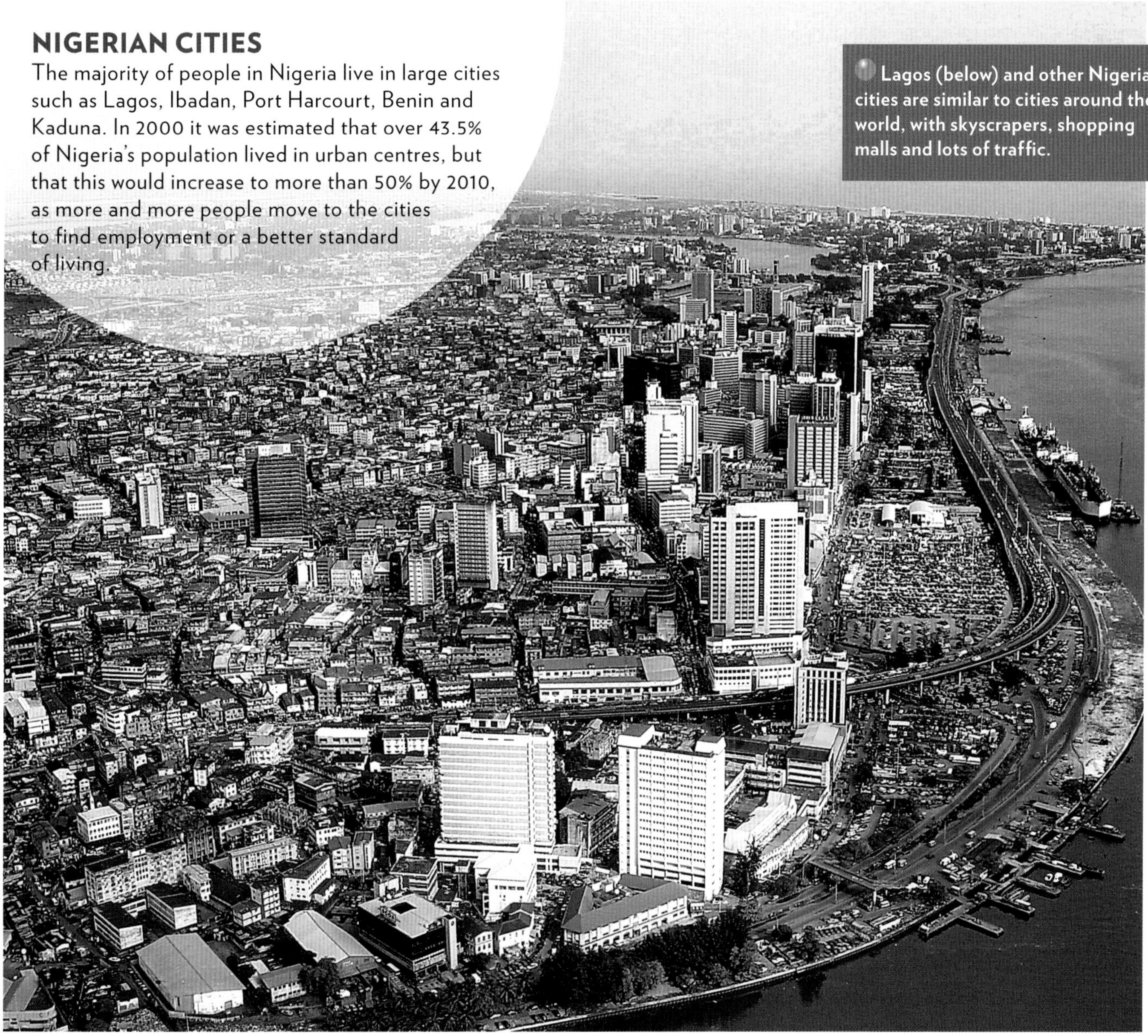

Lagos (below) and other Nigerian cities are similar to cities around the world, with skyscrapers, shopping malls and lots of traffic.

A landscape in Delta State.

# Differing landscapes

In a country as big as Nigeria there is a great variety of landscapes. Broadly speaking, the vegetation in the south is forest. Trees traditionally found in the forest include mahogany, iroko, obeche, oil palm, coco and rubber trees, and these provide some of Nigeria's main exports. However, the forests are being depleted because, for many years, trees have been cut down for fuel, for timber to export, and to clear the land for farming. As a result of this deforestation, many species of plants and wildlife have lost their habitats and become endangered.

In the north of Nigeria the land is generally flat, with low-growing vegetation. There may be no trees at all, or just small groups of trees dotted around. This type of land, called savannah, is where most of Nigeria's food is grown, including cassava, corn, millet, sorghum, wheat, cowpea, rice, yams and potatoes. The far northern part of Nigeria is also used for rearing cattle.

Savannah land in Kaduna, Northern Nigeria. Trees that grow on the savannah include tamarind, baobab, acacia and shea trees.

In recent times the north has been faced with another environmental crisis – desertification, as sand dunes from the Sahara desert have started to encroach on villages near the border and wipe them out altogether.

| WORD CHECK | |
|---|---|
| deforestation | removing forests, leaving the land bare. |
| depleted | reduced, or used up. |
| desertification | turning into desert. |
| destination | the place at the end of a journey. |
| encroach | to gradually spread into the space of others. |
| endangered | in danger of becoming extinct. |
| exports | products that are sold to other countries. |
| habitat | the place where an animal or plant lives. |
| plateau | a large flat area on top of high land. |
| savannah | flat land with low-growing vegetation, with no or only a few trees. |
| vegetation | the main type of plants that grow in a region. |

# Nigerian highlands

Did you know that the highest point in Nigeria is Chappal Waddi in Taraba State, at the eastern border with Cameroon? At 2,419 metres high, it is often called the 'Mountain of Death'.

Other highlands include the Adamawa, Alantika, Mambila and Shebeshi Mountains, also along the eastern border with Cameroon; the Udi and Obudu hills in the east; and Jos Plateau, which is home to several tourist destinations including Riyom Rock, Wase Rock, Shere Hills and Farin Ruwa Falls.

**The Dass Hills are in Bauchi State, which is also home to the Yankari National Park and the Wikki natural warm spring. All are popular tourist destinations.**

**La Campagne Beach Resort, Lagos.**

## DO YOU KNOW?

The pictures on pages 9, 10 and 11 show some different views of Nigeria. Which places would you photograph, to show a variety of views of your country?

What environmental changes are causing concern in your country?

# The Nigerian people

Did you know that Nigeria has the largest population of all African countries? It is often said that one out of every four Africans is a Nigerian!

From a census in March 2006, it was estimated that there were 140 million people in Nigeria. A census is an official count of all the people living in a country at a particular time. The government asks people to fill in a census form, which includes questions about the work they do, their age, and the religion and ethnic group they belong to. Can you think why governments need to carry out a census and find out this type of information?

The figures from a census in Nigeria are not exact, because people in many parts of the country don't like to give information about their ethnic group or religion, and some do not take part in a census at all. They remember that, in the past, governments gave different amounts of money to different states, depending largely on the ethnic group and religion of people in the state, and so some groups became more powerful in Nigeria than others.

Fulani women make their way to market in Birnin Gwari, Kaduna.

## DO YOU KNOW?

What is the population of your country? When did a census last take place in your country?

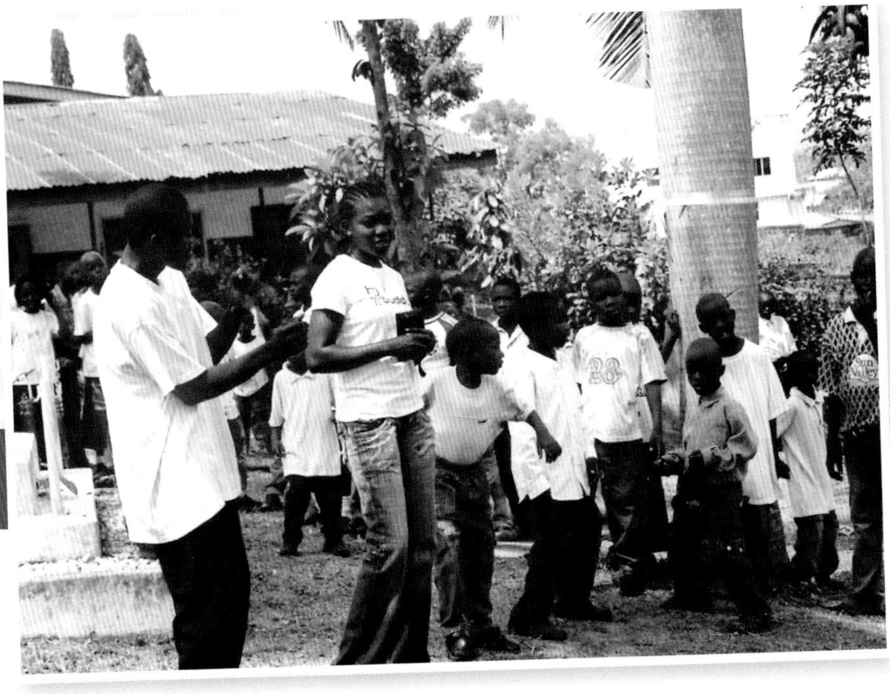

Children outside their primary school in Ibadan.

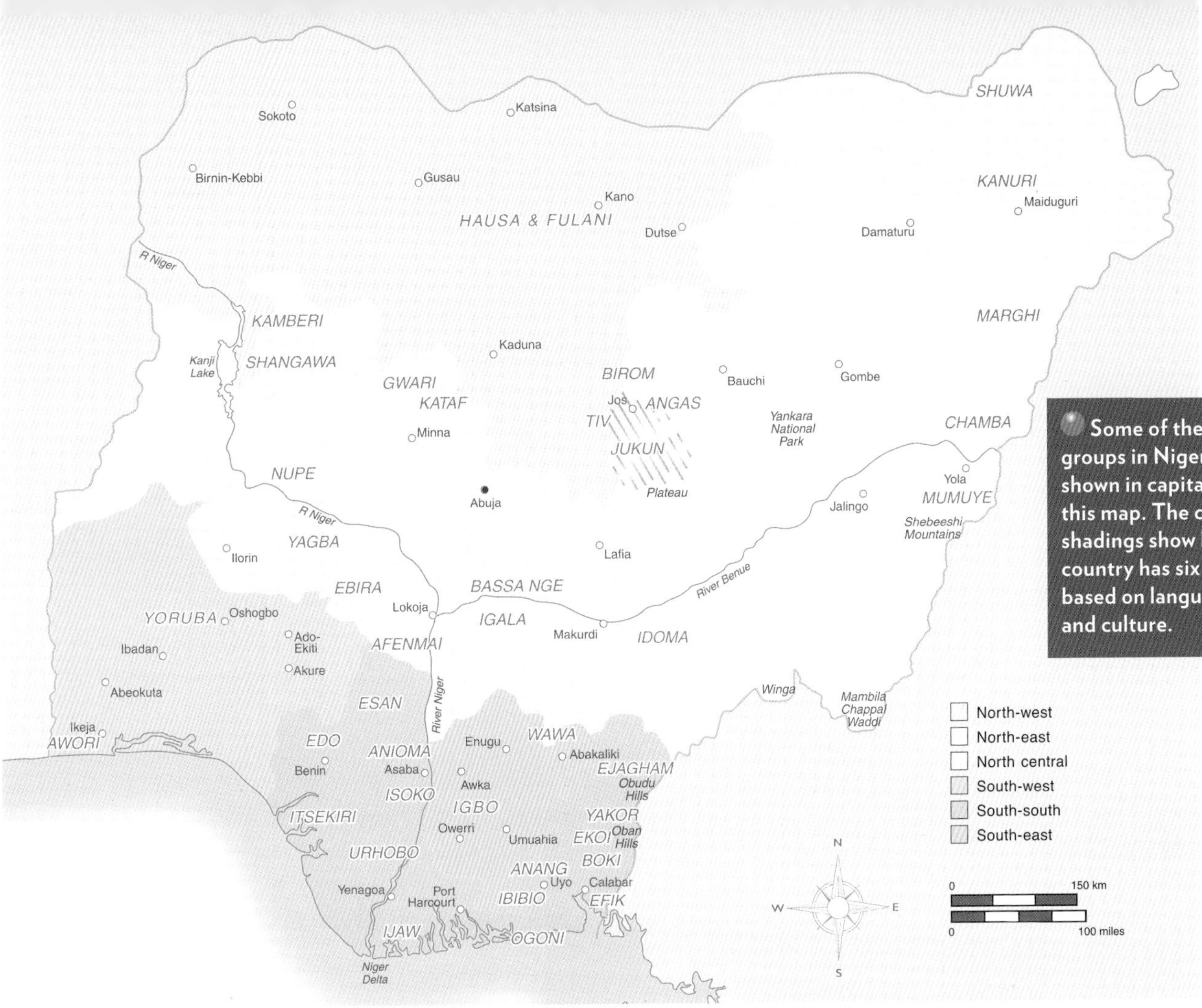

Some of the ethnic groups in Nigeria are shown in capital letters on this map. The coloured shadings show how the country has six zones based on language and culture.

□ North-west
□ North-east
□ North central
■ South-west
■ South-south
■ South-east

# Ethnic groups in Nigeria

Nigeria is a multicultural country, with more than 250 different ethnic groups. The three largest groups are the Hausa from the northern parts of Nigeria, the Yoruba from the south-west and the Igbo from the south-east. On pages 14-27, you will meet some Nigerian people from these three groups, and find out what is distinctive about them.

Other groups include the Fulani and the Kanuri in the north; the Tiv in and around Jos; the Urhobo and the Itsekiri around the delta of the River Niger; the Edo around Benin; the Nupe in the middle belt; and the Ibibio in Akwa Ibom state in the south-south region.

Tiv musicians decorated with cowrie shells perform at a festival.

| ✓ WORD CHECK | |
|---|---|
| delta | the mouth of a river, where the river splits into several channels. |
| ethnic group | a group of people belonging to the same nationality, or to the same race. |
| multicultural | including several cultural or ethnic groups. |

# DO YOU KNOW?

How many ethnic groups can you name in your country?

Which other multicultural countries can you think of?

# THE YORUBA

**Location:** South-west Nigeria and other parts of West Africa. Today Yoruba people can also be found all over the world. Large numbers live in Brazil, Cuba, Trinidad, the USA and the UK.

**Language:** There are several dialects of the Yoruba language. Some of the main ones are Oyo, Ondo, Ekiti, Ijebu, Ijesha and Egba.

**Names:** Yoruba names are often prayers and many start with 'Olu' or 'Oluwa', which mean 'God' and 'God Almighty'. For example:

Oluwatosin means 'God is worthy of praise'.
Oluwakemi means 'God protect me'.
Olubunmi means 'God has given me this child'.

It is common practice to address adults using the name of their eldest or youngest child. For example, you would call Bolanle's mother 'Mama Bolanle', and you would call Kunle's father 'Baba Kunle'.

Special names are used for twins or 'Ibeji'. The older twin is called 'Taiwo' or 'Taiye' and the younger is called 'Kehinde'. A child born after twins is called 'Idowu'.

## DO YOU KNOW?

In your language, what do you call adults, to show them respect?

**WORD CHECK**

| | |
|---|---|
| cornrow | a flat, tightly woven section of hair. |
| dialect | a form of a language spoken in a particular region. |
| rural | in or belonging to the countryside. |
| tradition | a custom. |
| traditional | following established ways of doing things, as in the past. |
| tribe | a group of people believed to be descended from the same ancestor. |

**Physical features:** Many years ago it was commonplace to cut tribal marks on the face and arms. The marks showed which Yoruba tribe a person came from. Nowadays the practice is dying out and is restricted to very rural areas or particularly traditional families.

Women and young girls tend to weave or plait their hair into elaborate cornrows, called 'irun didi' or 'irun kiko'. For these, the hair is parted into small pieces and black thread is wound cleverly around each part so that they can all be bent into different shapes to form different designs. Treating the hair in this way helps it to grow, as well as keeping it tidy. Although many women still dress their hair in this way today, it has become increasingly popular among the younger generation to perm their hair, or add hair extensions or weaves. Men and young boys generally keep their hair short.

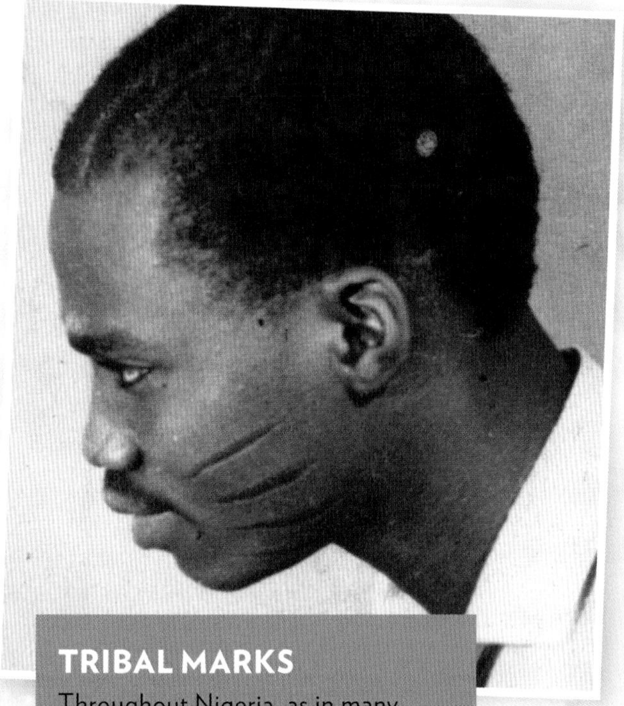

## TRIBAL MARKS

Throughout Nigeria, as in many other countries in Africa and some other parts of the world, there is an old tradition of cutting marks on the face, hands, arms or other parts of the body. The marks vary in length, width and depth and are cut with a sharp razor blade while a child is still young. For many people, the marks are purely decorative and a sign of beauty. They may show the family, town or ethnic group that a person comes from. Some are a sign of whether a person is married, or their religious beliefs, or their trade or position or role in the community. Today, except in very rural areas, it is not common to see children with tribal marks, because there is no longer a need for them and the practice is old-fashioned. However, body paint is still used among some ethnic groups during traditional weddings and funeral ceremonies.

**Alicia Keyes and Stevie Wonder, and many other celebrities all over the world, braid their hair into plaits and cornrows based on traditional African hairstyles.**

## DO YOU KNOW?

Can you think of marks that people in your community make on their faces or bodies today?

Can you name any other ethnic groups who decorate their hands, face or body?

Why do people have markings on their bodies?

# THE YORUBA
## CONTINUED

**Clothing:** The Yoruba are famous for their traditional fabrics, which include 'adire' or tie-and-dye, 'ankara', 'asoke', damask, lace and brocade. Nowadays many different types of outfits are made from these fabrics, ranging from caftans and casual wear to haute couture.

Traditionally, females wear a loose-fitting blouse with a low neck and wide sleeves, together with a piece of the same cloth tied around the waist. The blouse is called a 'buba' and the cloth is called an 'iro'. A 'gele' is cleverly tied round the head so that it sits like a hat, and an 'ipele' may be worn like a shawl or tied round the waist, over the iro. The gele and ipele are similar-sized pieces of the same fabric. Sometimes they are made from the same fabric as the buba and iro, but sometimes a stiff fabric such as asoke or damask is used. A gele and ipele made from asoke or damask are usually worn for outings or special occasions.

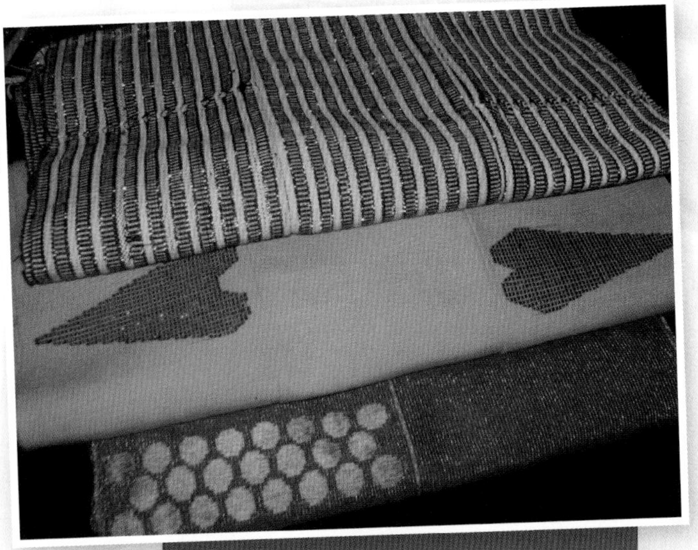

'Asoke' is handwoven into strips of fabric, about 6 inches wide, which are sewn together to make larger pieces of cloth. Traditionally, asoke used to be a plain, rich wine colour, often with little holes in it. Nowadays it is made in different colours and patterns.

This Yoruba woman wears a traditional head tie, known as a 'gele'.

| WORD CHECK | |
|---|---|
| caftan | a long, loose garment with wide sleeves. |
| haute couture | expensive, originally designed clothes. |

Sunny Ade is a popular juju musician. Here he is dressed in an agbada and sokoto made out of traditional asoke, to play at an event.

Males also wear a buba, but the sleeves are not as loose-fitting as for a woman's blouse. A male buba may be waist-length or ankle-length, and is worn with 'sokoto', which are trousers of the same material. An 'agbada' is a long, loose-fitting over-garment, usually, but not always, of the same material. For formal outings or special occasions, this may be worn on top of the buba, together with a 'fila', a traditional hat made of asoke or damask.

In modern times many of the population, particularly the younger generation, wear western as well as traditional clothing, and it is not unusual to see people in designer-label clothes, if they can afford them. Traditional clothing is usually worn for special occasions such as weddings, funerals and naming ceremonies.

**Food:** 'Amala' and 'iyan' are made from yam flour. The flour is mixed with boiling water over a stove to make a sticky kind of dough, similar in texture to mashed potato. When cooked, amala is dark brown and iyan is white. 'Gari' is made from cassava. It may be made into 'eba', which is cooked in a similar way to amala and iyan, except that it does not need to be mixed over a stove. Amala, iyan and gari are all popular dishes, traditionally eaten by hand. Bite-sized pieces are rolled into small balls and dipped into a vegetable stew, which is often mixed with dried fish or prawns and accompanied by a red, peppery, tomato-based stew with pieces of fish, chicken or meat in it. Rice may be simply boiled in water and eaten plain with stew, or fried with assorted vegetables, or made into 'jolloff', which is boiled brown rice cooked in a spicy, tomato-based sauce.

Amala and vegetable stew (top), and jolloff rice with chicken.

# THE YORUBA
## CONTINUED

**Food (continued):** Plantain is a cooking banana grown all over Africa and the Caribbean. It is rather similar to potato, in that it may be cooked in a variety of ways (boiled, roasted, fried, mashed or processed into crisps). Fried plantain or 'dodo' is often eaten with rice dishes and is particularly popular among children because it is rather sweet.

'Ogi', made from millet and similar in texture to custard, is used to wean babies. It is also a favourite amongst the elderly and people who are convalescing. 'Eko' is a solid form of ogi, like blancmange. It may be eaten with stew, 'akara' (fried bean cake) or 'moyin moyin' (steamed bean cake).

**Religion:** Christianity, Islam and African traditional religion.

**Culture:** Like most Africans, the Yoruba celebrate childbirth, and so naming ceremonies are very important. Traditionally, the Yoruba name their children on the 7th day after birth. Marriage and funerals are also widely celebrated and may last from a couple of days to a week or two.

A number of pagan festivals are celebrated every year or following a particular event. The Eyo festival in Lagos is in honour of the ancestors and involves a parade of men wearing flowing white robes and matching hats and carrying staffs. Each day, a colourful, masked dancer called 'Engungun' dances among them. The 24-day event usually occurs after the death of a traditional Yoruba leader called an 'oba' or chief, or in honour of a new one.

Masked dancers entertain the crowds at Tinubu Square, Lagos, during the popular Eyo festival.

| WORD CHECK | |
|---|---|
| convalesce | to rest and take things gently, in order to recover after an illness. |
| pagan | belonging to an ancient religion, usually one with many gods, that started before Christianity. |
| wean | to accustom a baby to food other than milk. |

## AFRICAN TRADITIONAL RELIGION

African traditional religion includes the worship of ancestors, objects and materials such as iron, and natural elements such as thunder, fire and water. It also includes magic and pagan worship.

Other festivals include the Oshun and the Benin festivals. Most Yoruba festivals are very colourful and there is lots of singing, drumming and dancing.

**Dancers from Benin at the Abuja festival.**

**The talking drum is played all over West Africa. Among the Yoruba, the smaller version is called 'gan gan' and the larger is called 'dun dun'. Apart from playing music, it can be used to send messages.**

The Yoruba are famous for their brass and bronze casting, textile industries and pottery.

**Music:** Popular traditional music includes palm wine or juju, afro beat, apala and fuji. However, today, the younger generation favour hip hop, reggae, jazz, gospel and soul.

**The calabash or 'shekere' is a shaker made from a calabash decorated with colourful beads or cowrie shells.**

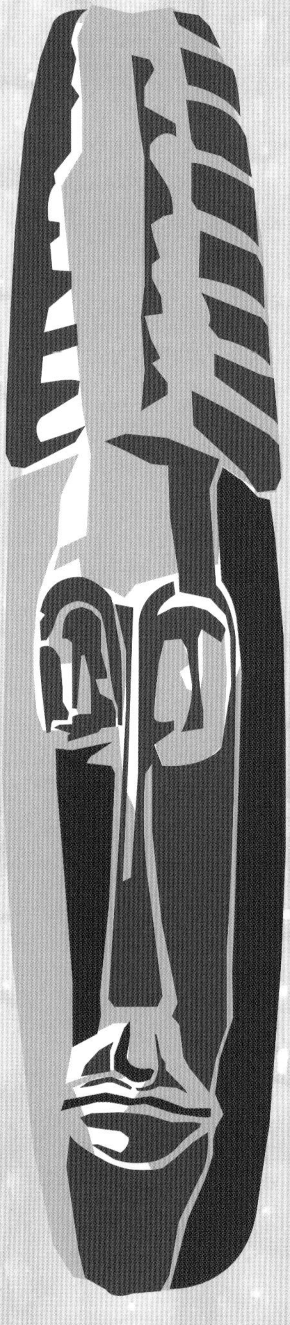

# THE IGBO

**Location:** South-east part of Nigeria and west of the River Niger. Like the Yoruba, the Igbo may also be found all over the world, particularly in the USA and the UK.

**Language:** There is an official Igbo language. The two main dialects of it are Owerri and Onitsha.

**Names:** Many Igbo names are prayers and are based on belief in God, called 'Chukwu' or 'Chi'. For example:

Chinwe means 'belongs to God'.
Chukwudi or Chidi means 'there is a God'.

Some children are named after the market day on which they were born. In the Igbo calendar, there used to be four market days per week, namely Nkwo, Eke, Orie and Afo, and each town or clan had its own market day when people would go to buy or sell things in the market.

Ekemma is the name of a girl born on Eke market day. Okoroafo is the name given to a boy born on Afo market day.

**Women buy and sell plantains at Onitsha market, one of the largest markets in West Africa.**

Red coral beads like these are commonly worn by traditional leaders called 'chiefs' and 'obas' (see page 18). However, imitations in different shapes and sizes are worn by male and female Nigerians on formal occasions.

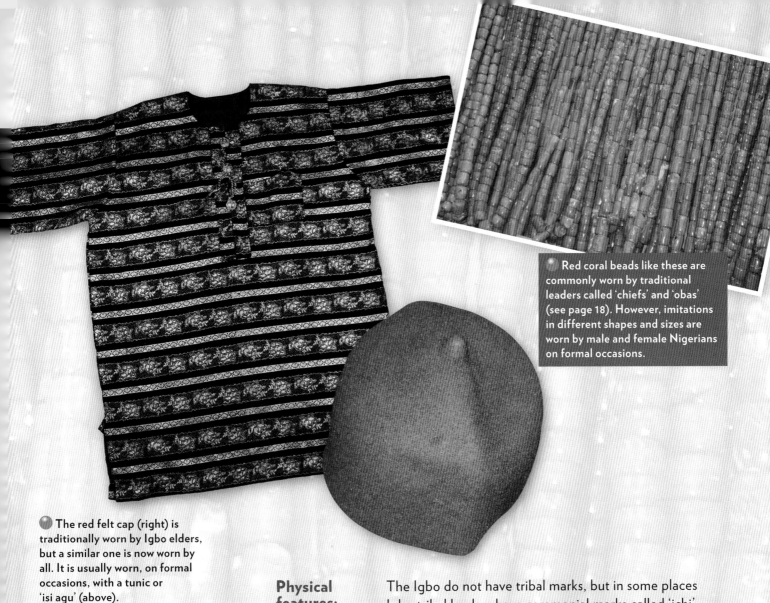

The red felt cap (right) is traditionally worn by Igbo elders, but a similar one is now worn by all. It is usually worn, on formal occasions, with a tunic or 'isi agu' (above).

**Physical features:** The Igbo do not have tribal marks, but in some places Igbo tribal leaders have ceremonial marks called 'ichi'.

**Clothing:** Traditionally, Igbo women wear a white frilly blouse with an 'up and down', which is two pieces of fabric called 'George', wrapped round the waist. They may also wear a scarf or gele called an 'ichafo'. They may braid or cornrow their hair.

Males wear a long shirt over a wrapper called an 'akwa', which covers the legs down to the ankles. On formal occasions they may wear a tunic called an 'isi agu', together with coral beads. They may also wear a hat and carry a walking stick.

**Religion:** Mainly Christianity. However, ancestor worship and African traditional religion are also common. The Igbo believe in 'chi', which is like a guardian. Someone who has lots of bad luck is said to have a bad chi. Someone with much good luck has 'a good chi'.

**WORD CHECK**

| | |
|---|---|
| clan | a collection of families, said to have a common ancestor. |

# THE IGBO CONTINUED

**Food:** Traditionally, the Igbo were mainly farmers. They grow yams and cassava, called 'ji' and 'akpu', which are the staple foods. Yams may be boiled, roasted, fried or pounded to make 'foo foo', a sticky dough eaten with vegetables, meat or fish stew.

**Culture:** A very important Igbo custom is for a host to present a kola nut (see page 23) to his guests. This custom is called 'oji' or hospitality. The host hands the kola nut to the oldest man among the guests, who then passes it to all the others so that they can touch it and offer prayers. After this, the kola nut is broken and shared round.

The New Yam Festival or 'Iri Ji' celebrates the harvest and is very important among the Igbo because yam is their most important food crop. During this festival only yam dishes are served, and the oldest man in the village tastes the new yam first. It is a time for merriment and making up. There is entertainment, including masquerades, music and dance, and feasting for everyone.

The tubers of yams (left) and cassava (main picture below) are used for food. They are carbohydrate foods. Did you know that Nigeria is the world's largest producer of cassava?

Among villagers, wrestling used to be very important. It is a popular sport and, traditionally, competitions were held in the village square to prove the strength of a particular town, village, clan or warrior. There would be music, drumming, singing and dancing. Wrestling was also used as a way of solving disputes in the community. Traditional wrestling is dying out and western styles of wrestling and boxing have taken over.

**Music:** Highlife.

## KOLA NUTS

Did you know that kola nuts contain caffeine, a chemical which makes you more active? Caffeine is also found in tea and coffee, and used as an ingredient in cola drinks and some medicines. Kola nuts taste quite bitter, but many Nigerians, especially the Hausa, chew them. Among the Yoruba and the Igbo, the nuts are also used during prayers at naming, wedding, funeral and other religious ceremonies. For the Igbo, sharing a kola nut is a symbol of hospitality (see page 22).

🔵 Kola nut trees are very large and grown all over Africa.

| ✓ WORD CHECK | |
|---|---|
| carbohydrate | consisting of starch, which is the main source of energy in food. |
| hospitality | welcoming and entertaining guests. |
| masquerade | a gathering of people in masks and costumes. |
| staple food | the main food eaten and the main source of energy in a diet. |
| tuber | a swollen part of a plant where the plant's food is stored. It is usually underground. |
| warrior | a skilled fighting man. |

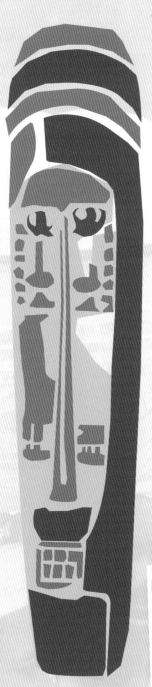

# THE HAUSA

**Location:** Northern Nigeria, Niger, Ghana, Benin, Burkina Faso, Togo, Cameroon. Some Hausa people may be found in Europe.

**Language:** Hausa and Arabic. These are the most widely spoken languages in West Africa.

**Names:** Many Hausa names are Arabic and come from the Muslim holy book, the Qur'an: for example, Yusuf (Joseph) and Yakubu (Jacob). Other names may reflect certain events or days of the week. For example, Sallau is the name of a child born on a sallah day (that is, a traditional Muslim festival), and Jummai is the name of a girl born on a Friday.

An elder twin is called Hassan, if a boy, and Hassana, if a girl. The younger twin is called Hussain, if a boy, and Hussaina, if a girl.

**Physical features:** The Hausa do not have tribal marks but some have Arab-like features and may be tall and slender. The women use lelei powder, which is another name for henna, to decorate different parts of their bodies, particularly the palms of their hands and soles of their feet.

**Clothing:**
Traditionally, Hausa men wear caftans. On formal or special occasions, they wear 'babariga', caftans with beautiful handmade embroidery round the neck. The Hausa hat, called a 'huluna', is also beautifully embroidered.

The Palace of Ado Bayero, the Emir of Kano.

Hausa women stroll in the market square.

Hausa women may wear a blouse and a matching wrapper called a 'zani', made from a colourful material called 'atamfa', together with a scarf or gele. Many women cover their head with a hijab, and some women are in purdah, which means that they cover most of their face too.

**Religion:** The Hausa are predominantly Muslim.

| WORD CHECK | |
|---|---|
| emir | a Muslim ruler. |
| henna | a reddish dye, made from the henna plant. |
| hijab | a type of scarf worn by a Muslim woman to cover her head and part of her face. |
| nomad | someone who belongs to a group of people who have no permanent home and travel from place to place to find new pasture for their animals. |
| purdah | in Hindu and Muslim communities, keeping women's faces veiled and keeping them away from certain places, so that they are not seen by men who are not related to them. |

## DO YOU KNOW?

Can you think of any special outfits worn by particular groups of people in your country?

Which group of women traditionally wear saris?

Which group of men are famous for wearing kilts?

## WHO ARE THE FULANI?

The Fulani are often found in similar locations to the Hausa. However, they are an entirely separate ethnic group and may be found all over Africa. The Fulani are primarily nomads and they consider their cattle, their most valuable possession, to be sacred.

The Fulani are generally tall and lean. Some may have wavy hair. The women use henna to blacken their lips and may have markings on their faces too.

# THE HAUSA
## CONTINUED

**Food:** Hausa meals often include 'tuwo', which is made from maize, guinea corn, rice or millet. Tuwo is served with a peppery stew, and a vegetable dish such as 'taushe', containing either sorrel or 'kuka' (made from baobab leaves).

'Koko', a porridge made from millet, is a popular breakfast dish, eaten with 'kosai', a kind of bean fritter. Koko and kosai are similar to the Yoruba ogi and akara.

'Furada-nona' is ground millet mixed with yogurt or milk. It may be eaten at breakfast, lunch or as a snack.

The Hausa are traditionally herdsmen, and so Hausa people in the north eat a lot of meat dishes. For example, 'suya' is a kebab of beef, mutton or chicken, with a hot and spicy seasoning, and 'balangu' is dried, shredded meat. It is boiled for a long time, pounded and then fried.

Suya is a very popular snack and suya spots can be found all over the country.

Horses are not common in southern Nigeria, but are popular in the north for polo and the Durbar festival, where lavishly dressed noblemen display their horsemanship on richly decorated horses.

## Culture:

The major Hausa festival is the Durbar, when the Emir, other noblemen and the army take part in a spectacular, ceremonial parade on horseback. As for most festivals, there is singing, praise worship, drumming and dancing. There are several other religious festivals as well, such as Id ul Fitr, which marks the end of the Ramadan fast, and Id ul Adha.

The Hausa are well-known for their craftwork, including leather tanning, pottery, wood carving, music and art.

## Music:

Music is very important among the Hausa and praise singing, a traditional male occupation, is quite popular. Many of the singers sing about particular groups or professions, such as the royal family and local doctors. Nowadays the younger generation listen to songs about contemporary issues such as politics, love and marriage.

| ✔ WORD CHECK | |
|---|---|
| Ramadan | the month in which Muslims fast, in daylight hours, and remember the origin of their holy book, the Qur'an. |

A Hausa man sells craftwork at the Federal Palace Hotel in Lagos.

# Family and home life

In Nigeria, as in most parts of Africa, children are thought to be a blessing and the family unit is often quite large. People think of their family as the extended family, which includes grandparents, aunts, uncles and cousins, as well as parents and brothers and sisters. In the old days it was not unusual for a man to have two or three wives and many children, all living in the same compound with one or more grandparent. In a wealthy family today, younger brothers, sisters, nephews and nieces may often be looked after as part of the household too.

However, things are changing, especially in the cities, and the family unit is becoming smaller. Some couples now consider two or three children to be the average number for a family, and women no longer want to share their husband with another woman. Nevertheless, it is still accepted that members of the extended family help each other out in every way they can, because Nigeria has no welfare system like that in many countries of the Western world.

● Children take a break from riding their bikes.

The practice of having more than one wife is called polygamy, and it is quite common all over Africa. Some Africans consider it to be a sign of wealth.

| ✓ WORD CHECK | |
|---|---|
| compound | an enclosed area containing a group of buildings. |
| welfare system | a system in a society, where the government provides health care and other social services for the people, using some of the money that people pay in taxes. |

● This Yoruba family are dressed in traditional formal clothes to go to a wedding.

# Housing

Like people all over the world, Nigerians strive to own their own homes, but there are some big differences between West Africa and Europe generally. If they can afford to, people in West Africa buy a piece of land and build their own home, rather than buying a ready-built house. However, nowadays, some wealthier Nigerians and those living abroad do buy houses already built, and limited mortgages are available. Building materials are different from in Europe too. In modern times, West African buildings are constructed with cement blocks, as opposed to bricks. The roofs are not made from tiles, but from corrugated iron, for people on lower incomes, or aluminium sheets or shingle, for people who are better-off. Furthermore, in West Africa, residential buildings tend to be brightly coloured and many have verandas upstairs and down.

In rural villages, it is still possible to find traditional mud huts, but you are equally likely to see modern houses of different shapes and sizes and at different degrees of completion, depending upon the financial circumstances of the owner.

**These are some typical modern houses and apartment buildings in Lagos. Construction is big business in Nigeria and a major source of employment.**

Did you know that building traditional houses out of red mud keeps the homes cool during the day and warm at night?

| WORD CHECK | |
|---|---|
| financial circumstances | how much money someone has and can afford to spend. |
| income | the amount of money that comes in, from earnings. |
| mortgage | a loan for a building. The lender owns the building until the loan has been repaid. |
| residential | used as homes. |
| veranda | a covered space outside a window, or along the side of a building, where you can walk or sit. |

**Outside a thatched house in Sokoto. The wall is made from mud.**

# Nigerian languages

Nigeria is a multilingual country. The precise number of languages and dialects is not known but there are certainly more than 350. Hausa, Yoruba and Igbo are the most widely spoken traditional languages.

## What's the official language?

The official language is English, which is spoken in government, business and schools. Nigeria needs an official language to unite all the different ethnic groups.

| ✓ WORD CHECK | |
|---|---|
| tense | a form of a verb, or 'doing word', that shows present, past or future. |

## Pidgin

'Pidgin English' or 'Broken English' is widely spoken all over Nigeria. It is a combination of native languages or dialects and very basic English. In Pidgin, compared with real English, it is not unusual for tenses of verbs to be mixed up, words to be spelt incorrectly or for a word to be used with an entirely different meaning. For example:

'Make you come ot there' – come out of there

'I de go market' – I am going to the market

'Demolish the dish' – This implies that you have finished your meal and thoroughly enjoyed it

### NIGERIAN PROVERBS

Proverbs are traditional wise sayings. In Nigeria, a person who quotes lots of proverbs is highly respected and considered to be very wise. Some examples are:

'A man's character cannot be washed by the rain.'
This means that you cannot change or improve a person's basic character, good or bad, because it is something internal.

'Truth is like oil. No matter how much water you pour on it, it will always float.'
This means that the truth will always come out, eventually.

'Do not tell a child not to touch a hot lamp. The lamp will tell him.'
This means that experience is the best teacher. Often children do not do as they are told until they have been 'burnt' or have learnt the lesson the hard way!

### DO YOU KNOW?

What does multilingual mean?

What is a dialect?

Can you identify some different languages or dialects spoken in your country?

Do you know any proverbs or wise sayings from your culture?

# Investigate languages

An alphabet is a set of letters that can be used to represent all the sounds of a language.

**The English alphabet has 26 letters:**
a b c d e f g h i j k l m n o p q r s t u v w x y z

**The Yorùbá alphabet has 25 letters:**
a b d e ẹ f g gb h i j k l m n o ọ p r s ṣ t u w y

**The Igbo alphabet has 36 letters:**
a b ch d e f g gb gh gw h i ị j k kp kw l m n ñ nw ny o ọ p r s sh t u ụ v w y z

**The Hausa alphabet has 28 letters:**
a b ɓ c d ɗ e f g h i j k ƙ l m n o r s sh t ts u w y ƴ z

The accents and other marks on the letters denote how the letters are sounded – for example, whether the sound is long or short.

In Yoruba, 'ẹ' is used when speaking to elders, people in authority, a group of people, or as a sign of respect, and 'o' is used when speaking to your peers or people younger than you are.

In the following vocabulary lists, you will see that there is sometimes no word in one or two of the African languages. In those cases, people most often use the English word instead.

## Count to twenty

| | Yorùbá | Igbo | Hausa |
|---|---|---|---|
| 1 | Ọ̀kan or Ení | otu | Ɗaya |
| 2 | Èjì | abụọ | Biyu |
| 3 | Ẹ̀ta | atọ | Ukù |
| 4 | Ẹ̀rin | anọ | Huɗù |
| 5 | Àrún | ise | Biyar |
| 6 | Ẹ̀fà | isii | Shiddà or Shidà |
| 7 | Èje | asaa | Bakwài |
| 8 | Ẹ̀jọ | asatọ | Takwàs |
| 9 | Ẹ̀sán | Itoolu/iteghete | Tarà |
| 10 | Ẹ̀wá | iri | Gwomà or Gomà |
| 11 | Mọ́kànlá | iri na otu | Sha ɗ aya |
| 12 | Méjìlá | iri na abụọ | Sha Biyu |
| 13 | Mẹ́tàlá | iri na atọ | Sha Uku |
| 14 | Mẹ́rìnlá | iri na anọ | Sha Huɗu |
| 15 | Mẹ́ẹ̀ẹ́dógún | iri na ise | Sha Biyar |
| 16 | Mẹ́rìndínlógún | iri na isii | Sha Shidda or Shida |
| 17 | Mẹ́tàdínlógún | iri na asaa | Sha Bakwai |
| 18 | Méjìdínlógún | iri na asatọ | Sha Takwas |
| 19 | Mọ́kàndínlógún | iri na iteghete | Sha Tara |
| 20 | Ogún | iri abụọ | Ishirin or Ashirin |

# Colours

| English | Yorùbá | Igbo | Hausa |
|---|---|---|---|
| Black | Àwọ dúdú | Oji | Baƙi |
| White | Àwọ funfun | Ọcha | Fari |
| Blue | Àwọ sánmọ̀/búlúù | Bluu | Shuɗi |
| Yellow | Àwọ Ìyeyè | Uhie | Ruwan ɗ orawa |
| Red | Àwọ pupa | Odo òdo | Ja |
| Orange | Àwọ ọsàn | | Ruwan Lemon Zaƙi |
| Green | Àwọ ewé | Akwụkwọ ndụ | Kore |
| Brown | Àwọ amọ̀ | Nchara | Ruwab ƙasa |
| Pink | | | Rowan hoda |
| Grey | Àwọ eérú | | Rowan toka |

## Now see if you can say some of these words in the different languages

| | English | Yorùbá | Igbo | Hausa |
|---|---|---|---|---|
| **A** | Ask | Bèèrè | Ajụjụ | Tàmbaya |
| **B** | Boat | Ọkọ̀ ojú omi | Ụgbọ mmiri | Jirgin Ruwa |
| **C** | Car | Ọkọ̀ Ayọ́kẹ́lẹ́ | Ụgbọ ala | Motà |
| **D** | Door | Ìlẹ̀kùn | Ụzọ | Kofà |
| **E** | Egg | Ẹyin | Akwa | Ƙwai |
| **F** | Fat | Ọrá | Ibu | Ƙibà |
| **G** | Glasses | Ìgò/Ife/Gágà | Ugegbe | Mudubin Idò/tàbàrau |
| **H** | House | Ilé | Ụlọ | Gida |
| **I** | Ice | Yìnyín/áìsì | Oyi | Ƙànƙara |
| **J** | Job | Iṣẹ́ | Ọlụ | Abin Yi/aikì |
| **K** | Knock | Kàn | Kụọ aka | Ƙwanƙàsa |
| **L** | Large | Tóbi | Nnukwu | Ƙato/bàbba |
| **M** | Market | Ọjà | Ahịa | Kàsuwa |
| **N** | News | Ìròyìn | Akụkọ ụwa | Làbaraì |
| **O** | Open | Ṣí | Mmepe | Buɗè |
| **P** | Push | Tì | Kwaa | Turì |
| **Q** | Queen | Ayaba | Lọọlọ | Sàrauniya |
| **R** | Robber | Olè | Onye ori | Ɓàràwo |
| **S** | Seat | Ìjókòó | Oche | Mazauni/àbin zama |
| **T** | Talk | Sọ̀rọ̀ | Okwu | Màganà |
| **U** | Umbrella | Agbòòrùn/Abùradà | Ọmbụrela | Lemà/Laimà |
| **V** | Van | Bọ́ọ̀sì | Ụgbo | Hayis/à-kòri-kura |
| **W** | Water | Omi | Mmiri | Ruwa |
| **X** | X-Ray | Àwòrán àyà/eegun | Inyo okpụkpụ | Hòton ƙashi |
| **Y** | Young | Ọmọdé/Ọ̀dọ́ | Nwata | Saurayi |
| **Z** | Zoo | Ọgbà Ẹranko | Ụlọ anụmanụ | Zu |

# Nigerian food

Nigerian food is generally hot and spicy. The staple foods vary among the different ethnic groups and include rice, grains such as cassava and millet, beans, pulses, plantains, yams, potatoes and sweet potatoes. All these are cooked in a variety of ways and are mostly served with meat, chicken or fish in a tomato-based stew. For vegetarians, there is a wide selection of vegetables, including sweetcorn, spinach and other greens, carrots, peppers, tomatoes, onions, egg plant and okra.

**PEPPER SOUP**

Pepper soup is very popular all over the country. It can be served as a light snack or a first course. It is very peppery and best when piping hot. Traditionally, it is made with assorted pieces of goat meat, but today it is also made with chicken and/or beef. If you do not eat meat, fish is a rather nice alternative. To prepare pepper soup, wash the meat, chicken or fish and cut it into bite-size pieces. Place in a pot filled with enough water to cover all the meat. Add lots of dry chilli pepper, traditional herbs, onions and seasoning. Bring to the boil until soft and tender.

## What's for dessert?

Traditionally, dessert is not common. However, nowadays, some families might have ice cream, tropical fruit salad, or cake on special occasions.

Tropical fruits include bananas, oranges, pears, pineapples, paw paws, mangoes, coconuts, cashews, guavas, grapefruits and melons.

Vegetables are plentiful and usually eaten fresh. This market woman is selling onions and greens, known by the Yoruba as 'efo'.

**DO YOU KNOW?**

What is the main staple food in your country?

Can you think or find out which are the staple foods of three other countries?

Which fruits and vegetables are grown in your country?

Which fruits and vegetables that you eat are imported from other countries?

| WORD CHECK | |
|---|---|
| imported | bought in from another country. |
| tropical | from the region of the Earth on either side of the equator, between the lines of latitude called the Tropic of Cancer and the Tropic of Capricorn. |

# Yam Porridge (Asaro)

Yam is a root vegetable, very much like potato.
Asaro is a traditional Yoruba dish, rather similar to a casserole with diced pieces of meat or fish.

**Do not try this recipe on your own. Make sure there is an adult to watch or help you.**

**Serves 2-4**

**Ingredients**

1 medium-sized yam tuber
1 medium-sized red bell pepper
4 ripe tomatoes
1 small red hot pepper (optional)
1 large onion
1 tablespoon of tomato puree
Cooking oil
Handful of dried or fresh prawns (optional)
1 dried fish (agbodo) (optional)
5 medium-sized pieces of meat or chicken*
Salt and chicken cubes to taste

*Fried fish may be used as an alternative to meat or chicken.

**Method**

1. Peel and cut the yam into medium-sized chunks. Boil them, like potatoes, with salt to taste, until soft and a bit fluffy, but still firm and with some liquid in the pan.
2. Wash the peppers, tomatoes and onion. Keep one tomato and half the onion to one side. Blend the rest in a food processor until smooth.
3. Add half of the blended mixture, the tomato puree, 2 tablespoons of cooking oil, the chicken cubes, and (if using) the prawns and dried fish, to the cooked yam, stirring gently.
4. Simmer the mixture over a low to medium heat for about 15-20 minutes, stirring it from time to time to prevent it from burning. This is the asaro.
5. Wash and season the meat or chicken, and boil until soft and tender.
6. Fry the pieces of cooked meat or chicken until golden brown.
7. Chop the remaining tomato and half onion and sauté them in a little cooking oil. Add the rest of the blended pepper, onion and tomato mixture to make a sauce. Then add the pieces of fried meat or chicken, and seasoning to taste.

**Serve each person a portion of asaro, together with some of the sauce. 'Wa bami re!' – which is Yoruba for 'Come and eat with me!'**

# Snacks

| WORD CHECK | |
|---|---|
| confectioner | a maker or seller of sweets. |
| processed | produced by a special manufacturing method. |

Traditionally Nigerian children eat a lot of healthy snacks, such as fresh fruit and crops of the season. These include sugar cane, 'agbado', which is boiled or grilled corn on the cob, 'boli and epa', which are roasted plantains with toasted groundnuts, and coco yam.

Processed snacks include plantain chips, which are similar to thick potato crisps, cakes, buns, 'puff puff' (like a hot doughnut without the jam), 'gala' (a particular type of sausage rolls) and meat pies. All of these are very popular. In modern times beefburgers and chicken and chips have been added to the list.

Boiled sweets, chewing gum, toffee and biscuits are manufactured locally, but a wide variety of sweets, chocolate and biscuits are imported from other countries.

Plantain chips (left) are made from unripe plantain. Fried plantain or 'dodo' is also very popular and sweet to taste. It may be eaten as a main dish with eggs or a sauce, and as a side dish with rice or asaro.

Mr Biggs is a major food chain in Nigeria. Its menu includes snacks such as cakes, as well as meat pies, roast chicken and ice cream.

Cadbury is the main confectioner in Nigeria. Apart from sweets and bubble gum, it also manufactures a chocolate drink called bournvita.

# Agriculture

In the 1960s agriculture accounted for about 60% of Nigeria's income, but then, for many years, the government neglected this part of the country's economy and made poor policies about it. Fortunately, today, farming is becoming important again and this has resulted in a reduction in food imports.

Farms are generally smallholdings, or of the subsistence type, and scattered all over the country. However, the government now recognises the benefits of large-scale agriculture and the need to improve and increase production of food for Nigeria's people, raw materials for Nigerian industry, and cash crops, such as cocoa, cassava and rice, for export. In the long term, action based on these ideas will help to create more jobs, reduce poverty and increase Nigeria's earnings from other countries.

Cash crops are crops grown for export, in order to earn income for the country. As well as cocoa, cassava and rice, cash crops grown in Nigeria include palm produce, kola nuts, cashew nuts, groundnuts, tobacco, beans, rubber, gum, sesame seeds, cotton and soybeans.

## DO YOU KNOW?

What types of farming are practised in your country?

Name a product from your country and three things that can be manufactured from it.

Can you think of a product grown in your country that is exported?

Can you name 3 products that countries other than your own are famous for?

A palm wine tapper scales a tree to collect sap. It is usual to leave a container tapped into a tree for three or four days.

| WORD CHECK | |
|---|---|
| agriculture | farming. |
| imports | goods bought in from other countries. |
| kernel | the edible part of a nut, not its shell. |
| policy | a rule that guides what can be done. |
| sap | the juice that circulates in a plant. |
| smallholding | a small piece of land, not as big as a normal farm. |
| subsistence farming | producing only enough food on your farm to feed yourself and your family. (Not producing any surplus food that can be sold.) |
| tapper | someone who gets sap out of a tree. |

## PRODUCTS FROM PALM TREES

Palm wine is Nigerian beer. It is made from the sweet, milky sap of the white oil palm tree, the male 'Abe'.

The female 'Abe' is called the red oil palm tree. Its fruit and its seed, the palm kernel, are used to make palm oil for cooking, which is rich in vitamins A and E. Palm oil is also used in making margarine and chocolate and in making soap.

The leaves of palm trees are useful too, for making brooms, roofing and mats, and for wrapping food, instead of using foil.

# Natural resources

Did you know that Nigeria is the largest oil producer in Africa and the eleventh largest producer in the world? Oil was discovered in the Niger Delta in the 1950s, but it was not until 1971 that Nigeria joined the Organisation of the Petroleum Exporting Countries (OPEC) and began to reap rewards from its oil.

Also, 76 solid minerals have been identified in Nigeria. They include gold, tin, coal, bitumen, lead and zinc. Mining of materials like these used to be a profitable sector of Nigeria's economy, but it was allowed to fall into decline after the oil boom in the 1970s. The government is trying to attract investors in the mines from all over the world. Roads and railways are being built, and electricity supplies are being improved, in order to encourage investors. It is hoped that mining will grow and become an alternative source of income for Nigeria, instead of its oil.

A lone male pans for gold. Gold mining is small-scale in Nigeria at the moment.

Port Harcourt oil refinery is in Alesa-Eleme, Rivers State.

## DO YOU KNOW?

What minerals is your country famous for?

Which countries are the world's leading producers of oil?

This storage tank for liquefied natural gas (LNG) is at Bonny Island. Nigeria has abundant gas reserves.

| WORD CHECK | |
|---|---|
| boom | a sudden increase in a business and the amount of money it makes. |
| decline | a state of decay or becoming less successful. |
| investors | people who put money into a business, believing and hoping that it will succeed and make them more money. |
| mineral | a substance that can be obtained by mining. |
| pan | to wash earth for gold. |
| sector | part of a whole (like a segment of a circle). |

# Sports and games

Did you know that football is Nigeria's national sport and that Nigeria's Super Eaglets won the FIFA (International Football Federation) under-17 World Cup, 2007, beating Spain 3-0?

Boxing, cricket, netball, hockey, basketball, handball, squash, tennis, table tennis and athletics are other popular sports. Swimming was not common until recently, mainly because there were no public swimming pools. Nowadays more people can enjoy swimming, as those who can afford it are building swimming pools at home and it has also become easier to go to the beautiful beaches or to pools at the growing number of leisure clubs and hotels.

**The Nigerian women's football team, the Super Falcons, celebrate winning the fifth African Women's Championship, 2006.**

## Children's games

Children play a variety of games. Outdoors, younger boys and girls enjoy 'Who is in the garden?' and 'Hide and seek'. Girls play skipping games, hopscotch and 'Ten Ten', a traditional game involving singing and some fast and fancy footwork. Boys play football especially, basketball, table tennis and a game similar to marbles but using pebbles, bottle tops or palm kernels.

Indoor games include monopoly, ludo, snakes and ladders, dominoes, scrabble, chess, draughts, cards and a traditional Yoruba game called 'Ayo'. This is a complex strategic game, rather similar to chess, and ayo competitions are held. The game is played very quickly and helps to increase mental arithmetic and strategic planning skills.

**Table tennis is a favourite pastime for young and old. It is often played outdoors or in clubs.**

## HOW TO PLAY 'TEN TEN'

This is a girls' game, but there is no reason why boys cannot join in. The Igbo call the game 'Oga'.

You need at least 2 or 3 players, but it is more fun with more.

The players form a circle or a line, and one person, the leader, starts by standing in the middle, clapping, and kicking out her feet very quickly in different directions. After a few minutes of showing off her fancy footwork, the leader stands in front of someone, who must then mirror her actions exactly. If that person makes a mistake, she is out, and the leader chooses a new person to stand in front of. If the person does not make a mistake and copies the leader exactly, then she takes over from the leader and the game carries on, with each leader performing her own special footwork, until the last person remaining wins the game.

In modern times, an increasing number of children are more likely to spend their time watching cable TV, videos or DVDs, listening to music on their MP3 player, or playing games on their computer, PSP, Game boy or Nintendo.

**WORD CHECK**

| | |
|---|---|
| strategic | to do with strategy, the skill of planning a way to win and carrying out the plan successfully. |

## DO YOU KNOW?

What is your favourite game at school?

Can you explain how the game is played?

Do you know any traditional games that are particular to your country, or to any other country?

## HOW TO PLAY 'AYO'

'Ayo' is a traditional Yoruba game, played by young and old in Nigeria and other parts of Africa. Among the Igbo it is called 'Ncho' and in Ghana it is called 'Warri'. There are several versions of the game. A popular one among the Yoruba is described here.

You need two players and 48 seeds

Each player has 6 hollows or 'houses' and starts with 4 seeds in each one. Taking it in turns, each player takes some seeds from one of his or her own houses and goes round the board, counter-clockwise, dropping the seeds into different houses until his or her hand is empty. Soon there will be some houses with only 1 or 2 seeds in them and at this stage each player can win the seeds from his or her opponent's house if the last seed dropped into it makes the total seeds in that house 2 or 3. As the game progresses, more and more seeds are removed from play and the game continues until one player is no longer able to move. The player with the most seeds wins the game.

**Ayo is usually played out of a carved wooden box or ayo tray, which opens like a case and often has a handle at either end to make it easy to carry. There are two rows of six hollows, and two larger hollows for the two players to keep their winnings.**

# Animals and birds

A red hornbill at its nest hole. Nigeria has 862 species of birds, some of which are endangered or very rare, and so birdwatchers visit the country from all over the world.

## Wildlife

Nigeria has a rich variety of wild animals, including baboons, gorillas, chimpanzees and drill monkeys, which are an endangered species (see page 10 and page 51). There are also elephants, buffalo, bushbuck, waterbuck, antelope, duiker, hartebeest, lions, leopards, cheetahs, wild dogs, hippopotami, crocodiles and warthogs. In addition, the country is home to a number of rare birds such as the Olive Pigeon and the MacKinnon's Strike, which can be found in the Obudu hills in Cross River State.

### DO YOU KNOW?

Which animals live in the wild in your country?

Can you name an animal or bird that is particular to your country?

Are there any rare breeds of animals or birds in your country, which need to be specially looked after?

Elephants play at the Yankari Game Reserve.

Cattle are reared all over the country, but predominantly by the Hausa in the north.

## Farm animals

Chickens are the most common farm animal in Nigeria and are found all over the country. Guinea fowl, ducks, turkeys, sheep, pigs, goats, cows, horses, camels and donkeys are the other main livestock.

In many parts of Nigeria, a person's wealth and status are still determined by how many cattle he or she owns. Cattle have always been very valuable.

### DO YOU KNOW?

What animals would you find on a farm in your country?

What are the different products that you can get from cattle?

## Pets

Pet ownership is not very common in Nigeria and is generally limited to dogs or cats, although some people are known to keep more unusual pets such as monkeys or snakes.

### DO YOU KNOW?

What pets do children traditionally keep in your country?

Which pet is often referred to as 'a man's best friend'?

In the traditional story of 'How Ijapa became bald', Ijapa tries to hide his food under his hat.

### FOLKTALES OF IJAPA THE TORTOISE

Long before pen was put to paper, the story of Africa, its people and culture was passed down by word of mouth, often by the older members of the community, outdoors by the fire, under the moonlight.

According to Nigerian folklore, Ijapa, the tortoise, is one of the wiliest of all the animals because of his wit and cunning. He is a trickster, always getting up to mischief. Tales of his numerous adventures were traditionally used to teach children about social behaviour, and every tale had a moral.

Today there is not much room for oral tradition, and stories about the past that have not been written down are likely to be lost, as children read to themselves, watch TV or use multimedia and mobile phones.

# Nigeria's flag and coat of arms

The Nigerian flag is divided vertically into three equal parts. The central part is white and the two outer parts are green. Green represents agriculture and white represents unity and peace. The flag was designed by Taiwo Akinkunmi.

The headquarters of the Central Bank of Nigeria in Abuja has Nigeria's coat of arms on it. The coat of arms is used as a sign of national unity, authority and state power.

## The Nigerian coat of arms

A coat of arms is a badge including special symbols, which represents a person, family, organisation or country. Nigeria's coat of arms is shown on the right. The shield, which is black, stands for the good earth of Nigeria. The wavy bands in white or silver represent the River Niger and the River Benue, which merge into one. The two horses are symbols of dignity. The shield stands on a wild flower that is found throughout Nigeria, the Coctus Spectabilis, more commonly known as ginger. The wreath on top of the shield is in Nigeria's national colours of green and white, and the eagle symbolises strength. At the bottom is Nigeria's motto, 'Unity and Faith, Peace and Progress'.

Look up your country's coat of arms or emblem and find out what the different features of it symbolise.

### DO YOU KNOW?

What are the colours of your national flag? Draw a picture of it.

# The national pledge and national anthem

A pledge is a solemn promise. In many Nigerian schools the pupils recite their national pledge as part of morning assembly or, in some cases, at the end of the day. They say:

*I pledge to Nigeria, my country,*
*To be faithful, loyal and honest,*
*To serve Nigeria with all*
*my strength,*
*To defend her unity*
*And uphold her honour and glory.*
*So help me God.*

Children take part in a parade in Eagle Square, Abuja.

**DO YOU KNOW?**

What do children recite at morning assembly in your school?

## Nigeria's national anthem

'Nigeria we hail thee' were the first words of the national anthem adopted when Nigeria achieved independence in 1960. However, a new anthem was adopted on 1 October 1978. Its words are shown here. Most Nigerians know the national anthem, which is sung at ceremonial occasions.

**THE NATIONAL ANTHEM**

Arise, O compatriots, Nigeria's call obey
To serve our fatherland
With love and strength and faith.
The labour of our heroes past
Shall never be in vain
To serve with heart and might
One nation bound in freedom, peace and unity.

O God of creation, direct our noble cause;
Guide our leaders right;
Help our youth the truth to know,
In love and honesty to grow,
And living just and true
Great lofty heights attain
To build a nation where peace and justice reign.

| WORD CHECK | |
|---|---|
| anthem | a song of praise and gladness. |
| independence | not being ruled by any other country. (Nigeria was previously a British colony.) |
| motto | words that show what a person or organisation believes to be important. |
| symbol | a simple picture or design, which stands for something else. |
| wreath | a circle of flowers or leaves. |

**DO YOU KNOW?**

Do you know the words of your country's national anthem?

Do you know who wrote it?

# Money

In the past, before money as we know it today, people traded their goods by bartering. This means by exchanging one thing for another. For example, in Nigeria, someone might have bartered a piece of fabric in exchange for some salt, or some glass beads for some yams.

Modern Nigerian money consists of Naira (N) notes and Kobo (K) and Naira (N) coins. The notes are for N10, N20, N50, N100, N200, N500 and N1000. From February 2007 there have been three types of coins, for 50K, N1 and N2.

Cowrie shells were the first form of money, or currency, used in Nigeria and the whole of Africa. They were introduced to the continent in the 14th century, by Arab traders, and were often used in exchange for goods along the trans-Saharan trade routes. Later, during the time of the slave trade, cowries were given in exchange for slaves.

Today, cowries are part of Nigerian wedding customs among several ethnic groups. Cowries are used as the dowry or 'bride price' that the bridegroom's family must pay to the bride's family before the marriage can take place. Cowries are also used as decorations on clothes and musical instruments and for playing various games.

These headdresses worn at the Argungu fishing festival are decorated with cowrie shells.

| WORD CHECK | |
|---|---|
| currency | the type of money used in a country. |
| exchange rate | how much one unit of a country's money is worth in another currency. |

In the 16th century, copper bracelets and leg bands called manillas were used as currency throughout West Africa. The value of a manilla was much greater than a cowrie. Manillas were often referred to as 'slave currency', though used to buy pepper, ivory and palm produce as well as slaves. The currency was abolished by the British in 1949.

When Nigeria was a British colony, the currency was pounds, shillings and pence. Nowadays the Nigerian currency consists of Naira (N) and Kobo (K). One Naira equals 100 Kobo.

## DO YOU KNOW?

The exchange rate at of the time of writing this book is N250 to £1. If you assume that £1 = N250 or US$1.50, can you work out:

How much will it cost you in Naira to buy a pencil case at £1.50?
If you started with £5-worth of Naira, how much will you have left?

How much will it cost you in US dollars to buy a book at £3.50?
How much change will you receive, if you started with £10-worth of US dollars?

# The climate

Nigeria lies between the equator and the Tropic of Cancer. It is a tropical country and is hot most of the year round. The climate and the weather are influenced by rainfall and humidity, more than by temperature.

There are two basic seasons:

The wet season lasts from April to October and is most apparent in the south, where annual rainfall can be as high as 400 cm.

The dry season lasts from November till March and is more apparent in the north.

The dry season begins with the harmattan, a dry, dusty wind that blows from the Sahara to the Gulf of Guinea. From then until February is the coldest part of the year. February to March is the hottest part of the year, when temperatures can be as high as 38 degrees centigrade.

## DO YOU KNOW?

Are there any seasons in your country? If so, what are they?

What factors affect the type of weather in your country?

The 'okada' or motorbike is a popular form of transport, especially when traffic jams and flooding during the rainy season make travelling difficult.

| WORD CHECK | |
|---|---|
| apparent | obvious, noticeable. |
| climate | the average temperature, humidity and weather conditions of a place. |
| humidity | the amount of moisture in the air. |
| rainfall | the amount of rain that falls in a certain period. |

# Major rivers

Did you know that the River Niger is the third longest river in Africa, after the Nile and the Congo? It flows through four countries, starting from the Fouta Djallon mountains in Guinea and passing through Mali, Niger and Nigeria, where it discharges into the sea through the Niger Delta. The Niger is 4,200 km long and joins with its main tributary, the River Benue, at Lokoja.

Other major Nigerian rivers are the Sokoto, Yobe, Hadejia and Kaduna in the north; and the Ogun, Osun, Osse, Anambra and Cross River in the south.

## Do you know?

Can you name a main river in your country? Where is its source, and does it have some major tributaries?

Timber is transported from Ekpe to the Okobaba sawmill, through the lagoon separating the mainland from Lagos Island. The sawmill is next to Makoko, a slum area of Lagos where wooden houses are built on stilts. The people who live here are manly fishermen, renowned for their smoked fish.

# The Kainji dam

The Kainji dam across the River Niger, and the Kainji reservoir, were built in the 1960s. As well as supplying water for people's homes, the reservoir is used for fishing, irrigation and transportation, and most importantly the dam's hydroelectric turbines produce electricity for Nigeria.

## POWER SUPPLY

Did you know that less than half of Nigeria has access to electricity?

Although Nigeria is the most populated country in Africa, the total amount of electricity it can generate is less than 4,500 megawatts, which is much too little for the country's needs. This has had a bad effect on Nigeria's economy as well as on people's lives. At the time of writing, there are 3 hydroelectric power stations and 11 gas-fired power stations, with more being planned. The government aims to increase electricity production to 10,000 megawatts by the end of 2007 and in due course to privatise the Power Holding Company of Nigeria (PHCN).

| WORD CHECK | |
|---|---|
| dam | a wall that keeps back water. |
| discharge | to flow out. |
| economy | how much money a country raises and spends, how successful it is at producing material goods, how much employment there is for people in the country. |
| generate | to produce. |
| hydroelectric turbines | engines turned by the power of water, which produce electricity. |
| irrigation | watering land for farming, by channelling water to it. |
| populated | lived in. |
| power station | a place where electricity is produced. |
| privatise | to hand over something that has been run by the government to an independent company or organisation. |
| reservoir | a large, man-made lake, for storing water. |
| tributary | a stream or river that joins and flows into another, larger one. |

A boat is moored on the Kainji reservoir, known as Kainji Lake.

## DO YOU KNOW?

How many electricity companies are there in your country?

Which types of energy are used to run power stations in your country?

# Transport

Many years ago, most people walked everywhere and a journey could take days, a week or even months. Sometimes people could travel by canoe, and in the north, some people rode camels or horses. In modern times, faster forms of transport include cars and other motor vehicles, bicycles, motorbikes called 'okada', trains, boats and planes. Motorbikes are very popular to help people to get through traffic jams more quickly. Traffic jams, called 'go slows', are common, because roads are not well-maintained and the cities are so over-populated.

Three types of transport are seen at one of the gates in the old city wall around Kano. The wall is a main tourist attraction. It was built in the 12th century to protect the city from its enemies. It is 14 miles long, with several gates.

## DO YOU KNOW?

What are the main forms of transport in your country?

What do people do to avoid traffic jams?

Above: Murtala Mohammed International Airport, Lagos.
Above right: A taxi park at Tafawa Balewa Square, Lagos. This square is also known as Racecourse.
Right: Cargo boats on the lagoon at Lagos marina.

# Occupations

Like most modern societies, Nigeria can boast of doctors, lawyers, architects, engineers, pharmacists and other professionals, but large numbers of them have emigrated to work in other countries, mainly because of concerns about Nigeria's unstable economy. When highly skilled people leave their own country for better-paid jobs elsewhere, it is called a 'brain drain'. Countries all over Africa suffer from the 'brain drain' and their governments are making efforts to attract professionals back home, to help to build their own economies which badly need their skills and services.

Traditional occupations in Nigeria include being a palm wine tapper, tailor, blacksmith, craftsman, leather tanner, herbalist, market trader, hunter and fisherman.

Hospitals, factories and building sites are three important types of workplace.

Beautifully patterned fabric is dyed blue and indigo at the Kofar Mata dyeing pits in Kano. The dyeing pits are said to be over 500 years old.

| WORD CHECK | |
|---|---|
| architect | someone who designs buildings. |
| blacksmith | someone who makes things from iron, by heating and beating it with a hammer. |
| emigrate | to move to another country. |
| engineer | someone who designs or makes engines or machinery. |
| herbalist | someone who knows how to use plants and herbs as medicines. |
| professional | someone in a job that needs a lot of learning and training. |
| tanner | someone who turns animal skins into leather. |

## DO YOU KNOW?

Which occupations are traditional in your country?

Do you have herbalists in your country? If so, what are they called?

# Tourism

Nigeria is a huge country, with much to offer tourists, but there is still some way to go before it features in travel brochures as an exciting destination like the Caribbean, Dubai, Kenya and South Africa.

Places of interest in Nigeria include the Obudu Cattle Ranch and Tinapa, a centre for business and leisure activities, in Cross River State; Olumo Rock in Ogun State; Yankari Game Reserve in Bauchi; Gurara Waterfalls in Kwara State; and the Slave Market in Lagos State. There are numerous festivals throughout the year, some of which attract visitors from all over the world.

Did you know that the Obudu Cattle Ranch has an international mountain race of 11.25 kilometres, up a height of 1600 metres?

A cable-car takes visitors up the mountain at the Obudu Cattle Ranch in Cross River State.

Rock formations like these are found all over Plateau State, which has the coolest climate in Nigeria. Plateau State is also home to Riyom Rock and Assop Falls.

## Do you know?

What are some of the main tourist attractions in your country?

Can you name three famous tourist attractions from around the world?

The Federal Palace Hotel at Lagos.

Drill monkeys are an endangered species and can only be found today in Cameroon and in Nigeria, at the Afi Mountain Ranch Sanctuary in Calabar.

People can visit the cells at the former slave market in Badagry, which was a major slave port in West Africa during the transatlantic slave trade.

The four-day Argungu fishing festival in Kebbi State has been held each year since 1934 and is a major tourist attraction. Thousands of men from around the world compete to catch the largest fish.

# Years gone by

**Notes:**
*Because some of the written records have been lost, some of the early dates in this Nigeria timeline are only approximate. Modern-day Nigeria did not exist until 1914, when the British merged two protectorates to form the colony and protectorate of Nigeria. (The colony gained its independence in 1960.)*

### 500BC-AD300
People called the Nok live in northern Nigeria.
(Artefacts including terracotta figures dating back around 2,000 years have been found in Jos. They show that groups of Nok people were settled at that time in the land that is now Nigeria.)

### 900
The earliest-known Nigerian bronzes are found at Igbo-Ukwu in the eastern part of the country.

### 500-1000
Hausa states emerge in northern Nigeria. They are never united but flourish between the 12th and 14th centuries.

### 1100
The Kanem Bornu Empire emerges around the area which is today Lake Chad, central Niger and Hausa land in Nigeria.

### 1200-1300
The Mali Empire extends to the north-western part of modern-day Nigeria, spreading Islam (the Muslim religion) among the Hausa people.

### 1200-1300
The Benin Empire in southern Nigeria. It reaches its peak around the 16th century.

### 1200-1400
Bronze casting flourishes at Ile Ife, in southern Nigeria, traditionally said to be the spiritual home and centre of the Yoruba civilisation.

### 1440-1880
The transatlantic slave trade. More than 12 million people from Africa are bought, in exchange for manufactured goods, and then sold as slaves in America, in exchange for sugar, tobacco, coffee and cotton, etc. The trade lays the foundation for the industrial revolution in Europe.

### 1480
As Mali declines, the Songhai Empire emerges from what is now north-western Nigeria and takes over as the major political power.

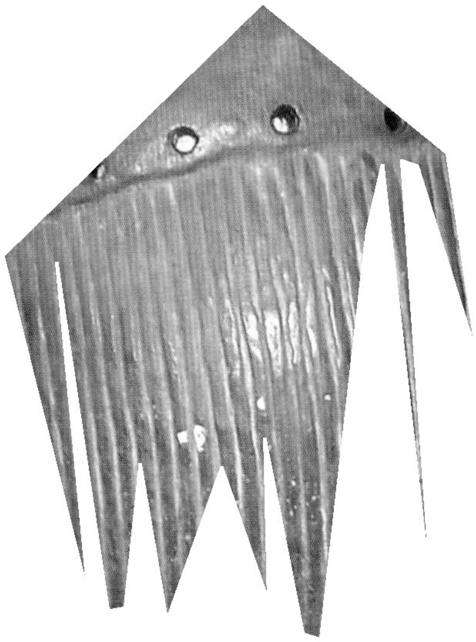

**This Ife bronze head of a man dates from between the 12th and 15th centuries AD. It is one of a collection of bronzes discovered in 1935 by a German archaeologist, under the Oni of Ife's palace.**

**1485**
The Portuguese are the first Europeans to begin trading with Benin in Nigeria and the first to introduce Christianity into the country.

**1800**
The Oyo Empire is at its peak. It declines towards the end of the century, as a result of civil war and the Fulani jihads.

**1804-30**
The Fulani jihads in Hausa land.

**1807**
Britain abolishes the slave trade.

**1884-86**
Various European countries make colonies of African countries. Nigeria becomes a British protectorate.

| WORD CHECK | |
|---|---|
| abolitionist | a person who tried to abolish (put an end to) slavery. |
| Anglican | belonging to the Church of England. |
| artefact | an object made with human skill. |
| civil war | war between groups of people in the same country. |
| doctorate | a type of university degree. |
| empire | a large group of states or countries, all under the rule of an emperor. |
| industrial revolution | a time of change, as more and more goods once made by hand are produced by machinery in factories. |
| jihad | a Muslim holy war. |
| linguist | an expert in languages. |
| manufactured | made in large numbers, often in a factory. |
| missionary | someone who goes to foreign places to spread his or her religion. |
| naval officer | an officer in the navy. |
| protectorate | a state that is controlled and protected by another country. |
| terracotta | made from a mixture of clay and sand. |
| transatlantic | crossing the Atlantic Ocean. |

## THE STORY OF TWO SLAVES

**Bishop Adjai Crowther**

Adjai Crowther was captured as a slave in 1821, but he went on to become a linguist, a missionary and the author of several books including a Yoruba dictionary and the Yoruba version of the Anglican Book of Common Prayer. In 1864, Crowther became the first African Anglican bishop and received an honorary doctorate of Divinity from Oxford University.

**Olaudah Equiano**

By some accounts Olaudah was kidnapped from Nigeria and sold as a slave at a young age. There is considerable debate about whether this is true, but it is not disputed that, as the slave of a naval officer, he was well travelled and had a good education. He bought his freedom, became a Christian and an abolitionist and played his role in bringing an end to the slave trade. His book, *Gustava Vassa the African*, published in 1789, is one of the earliest written accounts of slavery by an African.

## 1914

Northern and southern Nigeria are united as a British colony under Lord Frederick Lugard.

## 1960

1 October: Nigeria becomes an independent federation. Sir Abubakar Tafawa Balewa is the first prime minister.

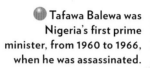

**Tafawa Balewa was Nigeria's first prime minister, from 1960 to 1966, when he was assassinated.**

## 1963

1 October: Nigeria becomes a republic, with three geographic regions. Nnamdi Azikiwe, former governor general, becomes the first president.

## 1966

In a military coup, the government is overthrown by Major General Aguiyi Ironsi.

## 1967

May: Nigeria is divided into 12 states.

## 1967-70

Civil war breaks out in Biafra, in south-east Nigeria, led by Lieutenant Colonel C. O. Ojukwu, who tries to break away and declare Biafra an independent state.

## 1975

Nigeria is divided into 19 states.

## 1977

Thousands of people from around the world visit Nigeria for the 2nd Black African Festival of Arts and Culture.

## 1979

October: Nigeria returns to civilian rule, under President Alhaji Shehu Shagari.

## 1991

Nigeria is divided into 30 states plus Abuja, which replaces Lagos as the new federal capital.

## 1992

Second period of military rule.

## 1995

Author and environmentalist, Ken Saro-wiwa is executed by the army, provoking international outrage.

## 1996

Nigeria is divided into 36 states plus Abuja, the Federal Capital Territory.

## 1999

Return to civilian rule. Olusegun Obasanjo is elected president.

## 2001

October: Obasanjo, Mbeki and Bouteflika launch the New Partnership for Africa's Development (NEPAD).

| ✓ WORD CHECK | |
|---|---|
| assassinate | to murder an important person, often in a public place. |
| Biafra | south-eastern part of Nigeria, inhabited by Igbo people. |
| census | an official count of a country's population. |
| civilian | belonging to normal society, not to the armed forces. |
| colony | a state or country ruled by another country. |
| coup | a violent action that results in a change of government. |
| democratic | in which ordinary people have the right to vote. |
| disputed | argued over. |
| Federal Capital Territory | Nigeria's capital, where the government has its headquarters. |
| federation | a united group of states. |
| independent | not ruled by any other country. |
| militants | people who take part in violent action as part of a campaign. |
| military | belonging to the armed forces. |
| NEPAD | New Partnership for Africa's Development, which was set up to support development programmes in all sectors of Africa's economy. |
| peninsula | a strip of land that juts out into the sea, almost making an island. |
| republic | a country ruled by a president, with no king or queen. |

## 2002

October: The International Court of Justice awards the disputed Bakassi peninsula to Cameroon, but Nigeria is determined to defend its right to this oil-rich area.

November: Hundreds die in four days of rioting caused by Muslim fury over the planned Miss World beauty pageant in Kaduna.

## 2003

April: Obasanjo is elected president for a second term.

July: Nationwide general strike. It is called off after nine days, after the government agrees to lower recently-increased fuel prices.

August: Violence between Ijaw and Itsekiri people in the Niger Delta.

September: Nigeria's first satellite, NigeriaSat-1, is launched by a Russian rocket.

## 2004

August-September: Deadly clashes between gangs in the oil city of Port Harcourt prompt a strong crackdown by troops.

## 2005

July: Paris Club of rich lenders agrees to write off two-thirds of Nigeria's $30bn foreign debt.

October: All 117 passengers and crew are killed when a commercial airliner crashes on an internal flight.

December: More than 100 people are killed when a passenger plane overshoots the runway at Port Harcourt.

## 2006

January onwards: Militants in the Niger Delta attack pipelines and other oil facilities and kidnap foreign oil workers. The rebels demand more control over the region's oil wealth.

March: Census.

April: Nigeria becomes the first African nation to pay off its debt to the Paris Club of lenders.

August: Nigeria hands over the Bakassi peninsula to Cameroon under the terms of the 2002 International Court of Justice ruling.

October: The Sultan of Sokoto is killed in a plane crash, Nigeria's third major civilian air disaster in a year.

## 2007

April: Elections.

29 May: President Yar'Adua is sworn in as president.

**This cartoon of Nigeria's New Dawn was drawn by Tayo Fatunla in May 2007, when President Olusegun Obasanjo handed over to his successor, Umaru Yar'Adua.**

### THE CARTOONIST

Nigerian cartoonist Tayo Fatunla published his first cartoon when he was 17. He studied at the Joe Kubert School of Cartoon in New Jersey and his work has been serialised by the BBC. He is the author of 'Our Roots', an illustrated history of black people around the world.

# Quiz Entertainment

“We have to be proud of who we are because it is our culture that differentiates us from the other cultures in the world.”
(Ara, 2005)

Sade

Seal

Sophie Okonedo

Ime Etuk

**The yellow buttons show the names of 10 Nigerians from the world of entertainment. Can you pick the right ones to answer the following questions?**

**Q1** Afro beat is the signature tune of which musician?

**Q2** Which female actress was nominated for an Oscar for her role in *Hotel Rwanda*?

**Q3** Which Nigerian both featured in and part-directed the movie *Crash*?

**Q4** Who produced and starred in the spectacular musical *Sundance* at the Hackney Empire in 2005?

**Q5** Who won the Best African Act award at the MTV Europe Awards in November 2007?

**Q6** Who won international, multi-platinum success with *Smooth Operator* and *Sweetest Taboo*?

**Q7** Which pop star is married to super-model Heidi Klum?

**Q8** Which talented female drummer collaborated with Stevie Wonder on his album *A Time 2 Love*?

**Q9** Which male model and actor starred in the award-winning film *Sometimes in April*?

**Q10** Which award-winning actor/film star played the part of Othello in the Shakespeare play, alongside Ewan McGregor and Kelly Reilly, at the Donmar Warehouse theatre in 2007?

D'Banji

**ANSWERS**

1. Fela Kuti 2. Sophie Okonedo 3. Ime Etuk 4. Patti Boulaye 5. D'Banji
6. Sade 7. Seal 8. Ara 9. Oris Erhuero 10. Chiwetel Ejiofor

# Quiz Science and technology

G.O.P. Obasi

“Learning and investing in science and technology are critical to ensuring prosperity and a high quality of life. Scientists are at the forefront of the development of innovations that can be used to solve problems.”
(Nelson Oyesiku, neurosurgeon, January 2008)

**The yellow buttons show the names of some well-known Nigerians in the world of science and technology. Pick the right ones to answer seven of these questions.**

**Q1** Which Chicago professor was named a MacArthur Fellow in 2005 for her research into breast cancer among African and African-American women?

**Q2** Who won the prestigious Gordon Bell Prize in 1989 for his work with parallel computers?

**Q3** In which year was the satellite NigeriaSat-1 launched?

Stella Felix

**Q4** Which 17-year-old Nigerian teenager was the first African student to travel into space?

Funmi Olopade

**Q5** Which internationally renowned pharmacist, head of the National Agency for Food and Drug Administration and Control (NAFDAC), is responsible for reducing fake drugs in Nigeria?

**Q6** Which entrepreneur is known as 'Lord of the Ring Tone'?

**Q7** Who was the Secretary General of the World Meteorological Organisation from 1 January 1984 to 31 December 2003?

**Q8** Who is the founder of the Global Women Inventors and Innovation Network (GWIIN)?

Bola Olabisi

**ANSWERS**

1. Dr Funmi Olopade 2. Philip Emeagwali 3. 2003 4. Stella Felix
5. Professor Dora Akunyilli 6. Alexander Amosu 7. Mr. G.O.P. Obasi 8. Bola Olabisi

# Quiz Sports

Kriss Akabusi

"Your success will be defined by what others say, remember and do as a result of meeting you and not by what you say about yourself."
(Kriss Akabusi, 2008)

Monday Merotohun

Hakeem Olajuwon

**The yellow buttons show the names of some Nigerians from the world of sport. Can you pick the right ones to answer questions 4 to 10?**

**Q1** What are the names of the Nigerian male and female football teams?

**Q2** Ijeoma Egbunine 'the Praise' is famous for which sport?

**Q3** Which sport do Christine Ohuruogu, Mary Onyali, Chioma Ajunwa, Fatima Yusuf and Beatrice Utondu have in common?

**Q4** Who was twice voted the National Basketball Association's most valuable player?

**Q5** Who was voted African footballer of the year in 2004 and 2005?

**Q6** This young man wears the no 93 shirt for the Chicago Bears

**Q7** Which famous table tennis player is famous for his backhand, and is now a coach?

**Q8** Which pair won the men's Long Tennis doubles at the Commonwealth Games in Sydney in 2006?

**Q9** Which former athlete went on to be a television presenter and motivational speaker?

**Q10** Which 'Nigerian Nightmare' retained his world boxing heavyweight title in October 2007?

Adewale Ogunleye

Jay Jay Okocha

Samuel Peter

Atanda Musa

Segun Toriola

**ANSWERS**

1. Super Eagles (male), Falcons (female) 2. Boxing (featherweight champion, 2006)
3. Athletics 4. Hakeem Olajuwon 5. Jay Jay Okocha 6. Adewale Ogunleye 7. Atanda Musa
8. Monday Merotohun and Segun Toriola 9. Kriss Akabusi 10. Samuel Peter

# Quiz Business and finance

Ben Murray-Bruce

"Give me credit only for what I've done. We did do something unprecedented in bringing debt relief to Nigeria. We broke the jinx and showed things can change."
(Dr Ngozi Okonjo Iweala, November 2007)

**The yellow buttons show the names of some well-known Nigerians in the world of business and finance. Pick the right ones to answer these questions.**

Ken Ife

Chris Aire

Charles Soludo

Kase Lawal

Donald Duke

Ndi Okereke Onyiuke

**Q1** Who worked for the World Bank before becoming Nigeria's first female Finance Minister?

**Q2** Which governor of the Central Bank of Nigeria was responsible for restructuring the banking industry?

**Q3** Which Chief Executive Officer (CEO) founded the Houston-based CAMAC International Corporation?

**Q4** Who is popularly known as 'the ice man' and famous for his red gold and diamond jewellery?

**Q5** Which female Chief Executive Officer (CEO) of Oceanic Bank International was awarded the Best Bank in Nigeria Award by Bankers magazine in 2006?

**Q6** Who joined the Nigerian Stock Exchange in 1983 and went on to become the Director General?

**Q7** Whose business enterprise includes sugar, cement, flour, salt and pasta?

**Q8** Who established Nigeria's first all-round entertainment company, Silverbird, which started with concerts but today includes cinema, radio and TV?

**Q9** Who was a governor of Cross River State and responsible for the building of Tinapa, a new world-class business and leisure complex?

**Q10** Which manufacturing chemist and educationist is a leading black businessman in the UK?

**ANSWERS**

1. Ngozi Okonjo Iweala 2. Charles Soludo 3. Kase Lawal 4. Chris Aire 5. Cecilia Ibru
6. Ndi Okereke Onyiuke 7. Aliko Dangote 8. Ben Murray-Bruce 9. Donald Duke 10. Ken Ife

# Quiz The arts

“Always try to be the best at anything you do. Even the best-paid footballers have to practise!”
(Chinwe Chukwuogo-Roy, November 2007)

Chima-manda Adichie

Ben Okri

Peter Badejo

Yinka Shonibare

Henry Oguike

Ifeoma Onyefulu

Chika Unigwe

Jeta Amata

**The yellow buttons show the names of 10 Nigerians who work as writers, dancers, choreographers, photographers or film-makers. Can you pick the right ones to answer questions 1 to 10?**

**Q1** Who was awarded an OBE in 2001 for his contribution to the development of African dance?

**Q2** Who was nominated for the Turner Prize in 2004 for his exhibition *Double Dutch*?

**Q3** Which Nigerian woman was commissioned by the Commonwealth Secretariat to paint a picture of HRH the Queen?

**Q4** Who wrote *The Famished Road*, which won the Booker Prize for Fiction in 1991?

**Q5** Who won the Nobel Prize for Literature in 1986?

**Q6** Who is the author of the novels *Purple Hibiscus* and *Half of a Yellow Sun*, the second of which won the Orange Broadband Prize for Fiction in 2007?

**Q7** Which Nigerian-Flemish author published a Dutch novel in 2005?

**Q8** Who wrote and starred in the Nigerian version of *Amazing Grace* which featured at the Pan African Film Festival in 2007?

**Q9** Which professional photographer is the author of several children's books including *A is for Africa*?

**Q10** Which Nigerian-Welsh dancer founded his own dance company in 1999?

**Q11** What type of work links the following people: Femi Elufowoju Jr, Tunde Babalola, Femi Odugbemi, Ben Onwukwe and Richard Mofe Damijo?

**Q12** Which area of the arts do the following people belong to: Baz Bamboye, Ronke Philips, Doton Adebayo, Adaora Udoji, Funmi Iyanda and Michael Okwe?

**ANSWERS**

1. Peter Badejo 2. Yinka Shonibare MBE 3. Chinwe Chukwuogo-Roy 4. Ben Okri OBE
5. Wole Soyinka 6. Chimamanda Adichie 7. Chika Unigwe 8. Jeta Amata 9. Ifeoma Onyefulu
10. Henri Oguike 11. Drama production and acting 12. Media and broadcasting

# Quiz Miscellaneous

Femi Oke

Obiageli Ezekwesili

Deola Sagoe

Emeka Anyaoku

“Africa today is a continent in transition and Africa tomorrow is a continent of hope.”
(Emeka Anyaoku, November 2006)

Tiwa Savage

**The yellow buttons show the names of some more well-known Nigerians. Match them to the following descriptions.**

Nuhu Ribadu

**Q1** Producer of the Element5 natural mineral make-up range

**Q2** A 'People's Peer' in the House of Lords since 2001

Adebayo Jones

Agbani Darego

**Q3** Two Queens Counsels (QCs) and Senior Advocates in Nigeria (SAN)

Ayo

**Q4** President of Nigeria in 2007

Toni Payne

**Q5** Former Minister of Education, appointed Vice-President for Africa Region at the World Bank, March 2007

Oba Nsugbe

**Q6** Holder of several awards for his fight against fraud and corruption in the Nigerian government

Fatima Usman

Umaru Musa Yar'Adua

**Q7** Elected the third Secretary General of the Commonwealth in 1989

Sola Akingbola

**Q8** The face of Magnum ice cream in 2006

**Q9** Was considered by many to be the favourite to succeed Pope John Paul II

Victor Adebow-ale

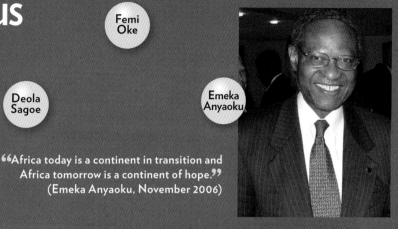

**Q10** The first black African Miss World, 2002

**Q11** An anchor with CNN and host of *Inside Africa*

Ola

**Q12** Three fashion designers

Prof. Fidelis Oditah

Cardinal Francis Arinze

**Q13** Four musicians

Yemi Oshunkoya

**ANSWERS**

1. Toni Payne 2. Victor Adebowale (Lord Adebowale) 3. Oba Nsugbe and Professor Fidelis Oditah 4. Umaru Musa Yar'Adua 5. Obiageli Ezekwesili 6. Nuhu Ribadu 7. Emeka Anyaoku 8. Fatima Usman 9. Cardinal Francis Arinze 10. Agbani Darego 11. Femi Oke 12. Adebayo Jones, Yemi Oshunkoya and Deola Sagoe 13. Ayo, Ola, Sola Akingbola and Tiwa Savage

# Further reading


Rob Bowden, **Africa (Continents of the World)**, Hodder Wayland, 2005

Rob Bowden and Roy Maconachie, **The Changing Face of Nigeria**, Hodder Wayland, 2004

Alison Brownlie, **We Come from Nigeria**, Hodder Wayland, 1999

Leila Merrell Foster, **Africa**, Heinemann, 2006

Esther Kerr and Yinka Ismail, **Welcome to Nigeria (Welcome to my Country)**, Franklin Watts, 2005

Lizzie Williams, **Nigeria: The Bradt Travel Guide**, Bradt Guides, 2008


## OTHER BOOKS BY AMLAP PUBLISHING

**How the Tortoise Broke His Back**

**Why The Tortoise is Bald**

## USEFUL WEBSITES

**www.amlappublishing.com**

**www.motherlandnigeria.com**

**www.tayofatunla.com**

**www.naijakonnections.com**

## NOTE TO TEACHERS AND PARENTS

Teaching and learning resources to accompany this book, including images, maps and quizzes, are available at www.amlappublishing.com. You may also email the author at info@amlappublishing.com with specific enquiries about the book.

# Illustration and photo credits

The maps on pages 6, 7, 8 and 13 were drawn by **PC Graphics**, from original templates provided by **Professor L. K. Jeje**, BA, PhD, Obafemi Awolowo University, Nigeria.

The drawings on pages 23, 30 and 55 are by **Tayo Fatunla.**

The drawing on page 41 is by **Lisa Parsons.**

The Amlap Publishing logo was designed by **Gary Pearson at Lomi Lomi.**

The author and publisher thank the following for their permission to reproduce photographs:

**Baffour Ankomah at New African:** pages 7 and 58 (Jay Jay Okocha), 17 (top), 56 (Ara and Fela Kuti), 60 (Wole Soyinka)

**George Ajanlekoko:** page 38 (bottom)

**Cadburys:** page 35 (sweets, bottom left)

**Pius Ekpei:** pages 7 and 57 (Dora Akunyili), 8, 11 (top), 13, 18, 19 (top), 20, 22 (right), 24, 27 (top), 29 (bottom), 37 (top), 38 (top), 41 (top), 43, 44 (top), 44 (bottom), 45, 48 (top), 48 (bottom left), 49 (bottom), 50 (centre), 51 (bottom), 58 (Samuel Peter), 59 (Ngozi Okonjo Iweala, Aliko Dangote, Cecilia Ibru), 61 (Agbani Darego)

**Olivia Essien:** page 28 (top)

**Mark Graves:** pages 19 (musical instruments), 21 (left and centre), 35 (top), 39

**iStockphoto:** page 42 (top left)

**La Campagne Tropicana:** page 11 (bottom)

**Mario Mazziol:** pages 10 (top), 10 (bottom), 12 (top), 25 (bottom), 37 (bottom left), 40 (bottom)

**National Portrait Gallery, London:** pages 53 (top), 53 (bottom)

**Nature Picture Library:** page 40 (top)

**Nigerian High Commission Library:** pages 42 (bottom), 52, 54

**Subomi Odunsi:** page 29 (top four)

**Buki Ogunyemi:** pages 12 (bottom), 33 (right)

**Remi Onigbinde:** page 36

**Bukkie Opebiyi:** pages 25 (top), 47, 50 (bottom)

**Funke Salako:** pages 9 (top), 16 (bottom), 42 (top right), 49 (top)

**Gill Shaw:** page 56 (Patti Boulaye)

**Shell Picture Library:** page 37 (bottom right)

**Muyiwa Sofowora:** pages 14, 28 (bottom)

**Paula B Sofowora:** pages 5 (all), 15 (left), 16 (top), 17 (bottom two), 21 (right), 22 (left), 23, 26, 27 (bottom), 33 (left), 34, 35 (centre right), 46, 48 (centre right), 48 (bottom right), 49 (centre left), 49 (centre right), 61 (Emeka Anyaoku)

**Mark Stratton:** pages 50 (top), 51 (top left), 51 (top right)

**Travel Images:** page 9 (bottom) (A.Bartel/Travel-Images.com)

**Special thanks also to the following for providing their photographs for the quiz pages:**
Kriss Akabusi, Alexander Amosu, Oris Erhuero, Lord Victor Adebowale, Adebayo Jones, Chinwe Chukwuogo-Roy, Philip Emeagwali, Nelson Oyesiku, Chiwetel Ejiofor.

# Index

# Index cont.